THE
GOVERNESS
AN ANTHOLOGY

EDITED BY

TREV BROUGHTON
AND RUTH SYMES

ST. MARTIN'S PRESS
NEW YORK

St. Martin's Press

THE GOVERNESS

St. Martin's Press, Scholarly and Reference Division,
175 Fifth Avenue, New York, N.Y. 10010

First published in the United States of America in 1997 by arrangement with Sutton Publishing Limited, Stroud, Glos, UK

Printed in Great Britain

ISBN: 0-312-21089-2

Library of Congress Cataloging-in-Publication Data

The Governess: an anthology/edited by Trev Broughton and Ruth Symes.
   p. cm.
  Includes bibliographical references and index.
  ISBN 0-312-21089-2 (cloth)
  1. Governesses--History. I. Broughton, Trev Lynn, 1959–
II. Symes, Ruth.
LC41.G62 1997
371.1--dc21   97-30125
                                                          CIP

CONTENTS

This book is dedicated to our parents:
Betty Broughton, Keith Broughton, Olive Symes
and Bill Symes.

LIST OF ILLUSTRATIONS

ACKNOWLEDGEMENTS

This book is profoundly indebted to the scholarship of, among others, Kathryn Hughes, M. Jeanne Peterson and Mary Poovey. In addition, we would like to thank the many people who have made suggestions and given help throughout this project: Bill Bennett, Joseph Bristow, Julie Charalambides, Simon Cook, Anne Digby, Mary Eagleton, Mike Farren, Trish Gannon, Judy Giles, Sue Grace, Robin Hart, Pamela Horn, Lionel and Maureen Lambourne, Jim Matthew, Jude Nixon, Gaye Ortiz, Helen Rogers, Zainul Sachak, Hugh Stevens, Patsy Stoneman, Naomi Symes, Olive Symes, Antonia Thompson and the late John Thompson, Philippa Tristram, Barbara Vaughan, Amanda Vickery, Cecilia Wadso, Jean Wall and Gweno Williams.

We are also grateful to Keith Parker of the King's Manor Library, York; the staff of the Special Collections Department, Brotherton Library, Leeds; Ann Dinsdale of the Brontë Parsonage Museum and Library; Véronique Gunner and Claudia Gold of Sotheby's, London; the staff of the British Library in both Boston Spa and London; Amanda-Jane Doran and Brigitte Istim of the *Punch* Library; David Whiteley, photographer, and the staff of the J.B. Morrell Library, York; the members of the Victoria List; Ronald Parkinson, Assistant Curator (Prints, Drawings and Paintings), the Victoria and Albert Museum; Veneta Paul, Angela Murphy and Jane Wess of the Science Museum, London; Margaret Dale, Librarian, Bear Wood College, Wokingham, Berks., and (with especial thanks) to Roger Tomkins of Stockwood Craft Museum, Luton, Beds.

The project has also received support from the Norwegian Study Centre, the Centre for Women's Studies, and the Innovations in Research Priming Fund at the University of York.

Acknowledgements

We would like to thank Cambridge University Press for permission to quote from Mary Paley Marshall's *What I Remember* (1949); Oxford University Press for permission to quote from Hilda Marsden and Robert Inglesfield's edition of Anne Brontë's *Agnes Grey* (1988); Allen and Unwin for permission to quote from Patricia Clarke's *The Governesses* (1985); Victor Gollancz for permission to quote from Alice Fairfax-Lucy, ed. *Mistress of Charlecote* (1987); Mr L.I. Baggott of the Schoolmistresses' and Governesses' Benevolent Institution for permission to quote from *The Story of the Governesses' Benevolent Institution* (1962) and to reproduce an engraving of 'The Home in Kentish Town'. We quote from *Miss Weeton's Journal of a Governess* (David and Charles, 1969) by kind permission of the publishers. We acknowledge Sigmund Freud Copyrights, The Institute of Psycho-Analysis and The Hogarth Press for permission to quote from *The Standard Edition of The Complete Psychological Works of Sigmund Freud*, translated and edited by James Strachey. 'Letter from Charlotte Brontë to William Smith Williams, 12 May 1848, Brontë Parsonage Museum, Grolier F3, is reproduced courtesy of the Brontë Society.

While the editors have made every effort to obtain permissions from all copyright holders, if any proper acknowledgement has not been made, or permission not received, we would ask you to inform us of this oversight, and we will do our best to rectify it.

INTRODUCTION

In a 'moral tale' for the young published in 1809, the heroine Ellinor, left fatherless and on the verge of destitution, attends her mother's deathbed.

> Ellinor burst into tears. 'Ellinor! Ellinor!' exclaimed Mrs Montague, 'destroy not by weak and childish complaints the hopes I have formed of your fortitude; repress your tears, my love; stifle your emotions; and listen with firmness to the dying words of your *Friend* and *Mother*. You know how incapable I am of leaving you a sum of money adequate to the necessities of life: you know likewise, that our family is what is called *great* and opulent; but you know not, my beloved, that there is no trust to be placed in relations: you must depend on God, and on YOURSELF for support; you must call into *action* the talents with which you are endowed; you must be *industrious*. Let not the proud name of Montague withhold you from pursuing any employment, however menial, which is *virtuous*: honest industry, my Ellinor, will add glory to any family, however great. You are now seventeen; you are blessed with a good constitution, good sense, and a good education: These are treasures of infinite value. To your care, Ellinor, I commit my poor Sophy; be to her a *mother*, preceptress, and friend.'
>
> (Mathews, 1809, pp. 6–8)

Entrusted with caring and providing for her younger sister, Ellinor immediately sets about securing an income. Conscious of her class origins and of her suddenly reduced circumstances, of the need to make the most of the 'cultural capital' of her education, and of the importance of honest industry, she gladly accepts an appointment as governess at Selby-Grove, a large country residence in the neighbourhood. The story takes a brisker turn as we follow her through the first hours and days of her new routine.

The morning after Ellinor's arrival at Selby-Grove, she commenced her task as governess. From seven to eight, the hour when the children were accustomed to take their breakfast, she appropriated to reading; the intervening time between that and dinner, was to be given to the study of French, the needle, &c.; the afternoon was dedicated to music; and the evening to rational amusement, instructive conversation, and healthful exercise.

When Ellinor entered the schoolroom, she found Lucy, Frederick, and Clara, waiting her coming; but Amelia was not there. 'Where is your sister, Miss Lucy?' asked Ellinor. 'I declare, Madam, I don't know; but I suppose in the garden.' A servant was dispatched for Amelia, who soon entered with a countenance beaming with good humour, and glowing with health. 'You are fond of walking, Miss Selby,' said Ellinor. 'Very fond, Madam: I detest the thought of being confined to dull study, while the weather invites one to the fields and gardens, where it is so delightful to skip and play with one's doll.' 'True, my love, all this is very pleasant when enjoyed with reason, but the distribution of our time is a duty we cannot too strictly adhere to. There are times and seasons for all things. To be idle and unemployed, is a sign not only of a weak head, but of a bad heart. And as it is one vile abuse of time which is given us for action, and action is of the utmost moment; so it is one sure method to lead us into other and worse abuses. For he who is idle and wholly unoccupied, will, ere long, be occupied in mischief. [. . .] Alfred the Great was one of the wisest, the best, and most beneficent monarchs, that ever swayed the sceptre of this realm; and his example is highly memorable. Every hour of his life had its peculiar business assigned to it. He divided the day and night into three equal portions of eight hours each; and though much afflicted with a very painful disorder, assigned only eight hours to sleep, meals, and exercise; devoting the remaining sixteen, one half to *reading*, *writing*, and *prayer*; the other to public business. So sensible was this great man that time was not to be dissipated; but a rich talent entrusted to him, and for which he was accountable to the great Dispenser of it.'

'Have you any more of these stories, Madam?' asked Clara. 'A great many, my dear,' replied Ellinor, 'which, during our leisure hours, I will repeat to you.'

(pp. 19–23)

Ellinor's curriculum – a little unspecified 'reading', French, music, needlework – seems, at first glance, to confirm our clichéd image of nineteenth-century girls' domestic education. Our folk-knowledge of the subject suggests that, for most of the century, middle- and upper-class young ladies acquired a smattering of ladylike 'accomplishments' and modern languages, and that these were usually imparted by an incompetent and demoralized governess. Yet what is striking about the passage is the no-nonsense way this heroine goes about finding work and managing her pupils. Clearly, in 1809, the now familiar figure of the downtrodden governess was barely on the horizon. Nothing could be more purposeful than Ellinor's manner of drawing her charges affectionately but firmly from mischievous chatter to serious discussion; harnessing casual remark to historical anecdote and hence to moral precept; demonstrating, even as she illustrates, the virtue of the rational use of time. Like many educational works of the period, the story depicts a governess in full command of her task: defining, generalizing, exemplifying, comparing, and forging robust connections between apparently disparate realms of knowledge. Her lesson ranges freely across time and space and from practice to precept. It is ingenious, economical, and above all, uplifting.

3

Fig. 1 The stereotype of the 'accomplished' young lady portrayed her as elegant, leisured and ornamental.

The very neatness of Ellinor's teaching methods suggests that the story is addressed to two overlapping readerships: an audience of children needing to acquire habits of study, industry and moderation; and a preceptress, perhaps not much older than her charges, who, lacking formal training, can nevertheless pick up hints about teaching as she reads the story aloud.

To a twentieth-century eye Ellinor's manner of instruction may seem bossy, impractical or just plain dull. Yet the unruffled self-possession of her first efforts as a governess reminds us that she was the beneficiary of a long-standing interest in how the human mind worked and how children learned. Indeed, eighteenth-century philosophical ideas about the nature of the 'mind' had, in the last decades of the eighteenth century, played an important part in validating women's endeavours in the field of education, and in formulating teaching methods that were to be influential well into the Victorian era. The preceptress was, in fact, a key figure in the application of Enlightenment thought to women and children. Her rational spirit haunts Maria and Richard Lovell Edgeworth's *Practical Education* (1798), for example, as well as the writings of Anna Laetitia Barbauld (1743–1825) and Mary Wollstonecraft (1759–1797). Nor was her influence restricted to writers of a rationalist tendency: evangelical educationalists such as Hannah More (1745–1833) and Sarah Trimmer (1741–1810) placed versions of her rôle at the centre of their educational programmes. Venerated by both traditions alike, she provided an organizing presence and a voice of authority to countless educational novels and children's books published around this time.

From the late eighteenth century onwards, girls' education had been the subject of fierce debate as philosophers and educationalists strove to define the best way of transforming young females into worthy helpmeets and rational companions. Nor was this envisaged as primarily an ornamental role: the best of husbands would sometimes be grateful for wise counsel and sympathy. Motherhood was itself a grave responsibility. The assumption that girls should be educated *at least* sufficiently to instruct their own daughters and prepare their sons for school guaranteed a high premium on effective instruction and encouraged that sophisticated 'dual' mode of address we have found in Ellinor's narrative. Foreseeing, like Ellinor's mother, that many young ladies might have to rely on their own 'industry' at some time or another, most educational commentators advocated a balance between pleasing accomplishments – music, drawing, embroidery and the like – and more straightforwardly academic subjects such as history and arithmetic. Whether carried out by a mother, aunt, elder sister or paid teacher, the role of 'preceptress' was thus an honourable one, vital not just to the respectability, but also to the moral stature of the family as a whole. Inculcating sound principles, industrious habits and polite manners, she helped to bridge the gap between generations and to ensure the passage of girls into rational, capable womanhood.

Ellinor's effortless entry into paid teaching, then, reminds us that the education of children and elder daughters was considered at this time to be the lifeblood of genteel domesticity. This was a world in which childhood was beginning to be valued for its own sake rather than simply as a prelude to adulthood; in which toys and entertainment had a place, albeit a carefully regulated one, within the schoolroom. Ellinor's story was itself part of a great burgeoning of writing for children, encompassing instructive verse, simple hymns, question-and-answer routines, and tales like this one, punctuated by pungent moral aphorisms and telling illustrations.

The frontispiece to this tiny volume reinforces the message that Ellinor as governess could regard herself as a central rather than marginal figure in well-bred society. Unabashed by the opulent surroundings in which she finds herself (her schoolroom is large, airy and elegantly equipped with books and globes), Ellinor sits reading aloud to her charges, the embodiment of dignity and authority. The attitudes of the four children express both deference and affection, and the whole composition exudes an atmosphere of earnest study. The picture owes much to the iconography of the family portrait, underlining the point that the roles of mother and teacher dovetailed at this time and that, in the early years of the century, the ideal governess was, indeed, 'mother, preceptress, and friend'.

Fig. 2 The frontispiece to *Ellinor: The Young Governess* (1809). (The original book is a fraction of this size.)

Frontispiece to "Flowers of Instruction."

What *is* so hateful to the sight.
What can so soon deform
Features intended to delight.
As passion's angry storm!

Fig. 3 A pupil learns to watch his temper.

The figure of the preceptress, with her highly developed reasoning powers, her elaborate repertoire of teaching skills, and her pivotal role in the reproduction of the genteel household, was to retain an important role in the nineteenth-century educational scene – whether through the influence of books in which she appeared and which retained their appeal for decades, through her impact on the childhoods of eminent Victorians, or through the survival of educational practices that would come to seem quaint and outdated. Her most important legacy, however, is more diffuse, and is to be found wherever nineteenth-century governesses and educationalists describe the business of teaching and learning: in their emphasis on sound habits of mind and on the cultivation of the powers of reason and observation; and in the simplicity and practicality of the methods they advocate.

Rightly or wrongly, however, the idea of the preceptress soon yielded in the popular imagination to a far more enigmatic, and, as it turns out, more durable image of governessing. It is a spectre liminally present in Ellinor's story, but firmly dismissed by her mother: that of the needy gentlewoman for whom paid employment means loss of caste and exploitation by inferiors. This image drew on, and in turn helped to maintain, increasingly rigid ideals of middle-class women's immunity from the toils of commerce. And because it played to profound beliefs and equally profound fears, it succeeded in displacing the more pragmatic, businesslike model of preceptress embodied in Ellinor.

The contrast between the two 'types' tells us much about changing understandings of the role of governess. Where Ellinor could adopt many facets of the maternal role without perceptible conflict, for the Victorian governess the boundary between teacher and mother was represented as a source of tension and rivalry. Where the former's pupils respected her as they would a revered aunt, the latter's might condescend to or even insult her. Where Mrs Montague would warn against reliance on relatives, convinced that 'honest industry' would be highly esteemed regardless of class or gender, a disapproving question mark would soon hover above any middle-class woman who chose paid employment over even the most servile and begrudging dependency. Where Ellinor could be confident that a 'good constitution, good sense, and a good education' were qualifications enough for the education of the young, her nineteenth-century successor would frequently find herself accused of inadequate training and hence of giving poor value for money. And because of all this, where Ellinor could command a salary sufficient to her own needs and those of her dependent sister, her Victorian equivalent would be offered the most meagre recompense, and sometimes no more than board and lodging for the duration.

It was this dispossessed, dispirited governess who, by the mid-century, was taking centre stage in the popular imagination and whose predicament was scandalizing a generation. Mary Poovey has argued persuasively that Victorian concern for the 'plight' of the governess was at least as much a symptom of anxiety about the 'erosion of middle-class assumptions and values' in the economically precarious 1840s as it was an outpouring of sympathy for the governesses themselves. (1989, p. 127). However one looks at it, one faces the sobering fact that the representation of governesses in print – in all its forms – was out of proportion to the number of self-identified governesses. As Kathryn Hughes and others have pointed out (1993, p. xi), even when the 'Governess Problem' was at its mid-century height, no more than 25,000 governesses registered as such in the 1851 National Census – one thirtieth of the number of female domestic servants, to make an obvious comparison.

What had happened to turn governessing from a convenient social expedient into a pressing national 'issue'? To begin to understand this we need to step back from the trials of individuals in order to focus on wider social currents.

A key factor was that single educated women had come to be seen as *literally* superfluous. Demographic factors such as mass male emigration to the colonies threatened to transform the usual slight numerical superiority of women in the population into (what could be seen as) a serious imbalance. This, added to the trend for late marriages had, by 1851, generated a 'surplus' of three quarters of a million involuntary 'spinsters'. It was a state of things, according to W.R. Greg, 'indicative of an unwholesome social state, and [. . .] productive and prognostic of much wretchedness and wrong' (1862, p. 436). And, although historians have subsequently disputed this, there existed an ineradicable impression that these women were disproportionately of the middle and upper classes, and that they were a burden to themselves and society.

The problem of what to do with these 'redundant' women greatly exercised the minds of the bourgeoisie, for whom the whole question of femininity was a troubling ideological crux. Newly emergent as a force in society, the middling classes deployed an elaborate ideal of cultivated domesticity in order to shore up their hard-earned and precarious respectability. The resultant 'separation of spheres', which increasingly took men away from home to make money, and fixed women in the home to show off that money, had a resounding impact on the way gender roles were organized and reproduced. An educational ideal emerged which was designed sharply to distinguish 'ladies' from working women, and 'feminine' acquirements from 'manly' credentials. The resulting curriculum, though less obviously 'academic' – read 'classical' – than boys' schooling, and less directly useful than what had gone before, was nonetheless arguably as various, as difficult to learn and certainly as challenging to impart as any other specialist education. Where maternal expertise was lacking, and where a couple of years in one of the small 'ladies' academies' was thought to be too expensive, too 'coarsening' or simply too impractical, then the kind of private education hitherto enjoyed only by the highest ranks of society now became appealing to a broader spectrum of potential employers. As Pamela Horn has shown, the class of householders keen to appoint a governess expanded to include merchants, important shopkeepers, industrialists and army officers. Farmers too, either because of their geographical isolation or to keep their daughters apart from their labourers, might consider it expedient to hire a resident teacher (Horn, 1989, p. 333). The governess came into her own.

The spectacular economic expansionism that allowed more households to aspire to the services of a governess brought in its wake equally spectacular failures, as risky investments and overextended credit led to bankruptcies and sudden penury. These, along with other catastrophes such as bereavement and desertion, ensured that the market was overstocked with educated single or widowed ladies seeking posts. By the accession of Victoria a rapid constriction of the kinds of paid work thought proper and respectable for middle-class women meant that governessing was one of the few options left open. This change in the relationship between femininity and work had harsh material consequences for ladies who found themselves without a solvent husband, father or brother to depend on. It also had psychological consequences for those for whom the delights of domesticity, the rounds of visits, and the challenges of philanthropy and household management were not enough.

It was the pseudo-domestic character of governessing, needless to say, that rendered it sufficiently respectable to be considered by ladies of refinement. (Needlework, the most eligible alternative, was if anything even more savagely exploited than private teaching.) However, cut off from the mainstream of educational reform, the governess found herself lacking the paper credentials and professional solidarity which might have bolstered her value in a fiercely competitive, overcrowded marketplace. Although state interventions in schooling for working-class children, the reorganization of nursing, mounting levels of bureaucracy and the growth of the charitable and public sectors gradually opened up new opportunities for middle-class women, the governess remained a vulnerable and isolated actor in the landscape of employment, and thus retained her hold on the British imagination even into the twentieth century.

Nineteenth-century writing about the governess is inexhaustibly rich; we have aimed to provide a varied and vivid sample. Like all anthologists, however, we have had to make painful decisions. The mid-century 'Governess Question' – the controversy over the fate of the female domestic teacher in an economically precarious, class-riven society – prompted many of the ablest writers of the day to speak out on her behalf. We have dipped into this debate in Chapters 3 and 4, but much remains unsaid. In Chapter 6 Wilkie Collins's Miss Gwilt (from his novel *Armadale* of 1866) must stand for a generation of tormented anti-heroines: Isabel Vane in Mrs Henry Wood's *East Lynne* (1861), the eponymous heroine of Mary Elizabeth Braddon's *Lady Audley's Secret* (1862), to cite but the more obvious. Even so-called 'classics' have slipped through the net: Dickens's *Martin Chuzzlewit* (1843–44), Elizabeth Barrett Browning's *Aurora Leigh* (1857), Sheridan Le Fanu's *Uncle Silas* (1864). Twentieth-century images of the Victorian governess – in Rachel Ferguson's *The Brontës Went to Woolworth's* (1931), for instance, or Elizabeth Taylor's *Palladian* (1946), or in the various productions of *The King and I* – are worthy of a study in themselves, but have proved beyond the capacity of this book.

Surveying the range of evidence at our disposal, it is difficult to tell how far the Victorian debate about the 'Governess Question' represented the interests and concerns of the teachers themselves and how far it reflected more diffuse anxieties about, and contradictions within, the constitution of gender and class. None of this, of course, makes the governess any less fascinating in herself, nor any less revealing of the preoccupations of her era. It simply means that we, as late twentieth-century readers, must take care to weigh each piece of evidence, taking into account its intended audience, its *raison d'être*, and the generic codes on which it draws. Apparently 'documentary' sources, for example, are often profoundly indebted to the literary techniques and conventions of melodrama, romance or travelogue. The novelists who depicted the governess life may have had precious little knowledge of its practicalities; those, like Charlotte Brontë, who did have such experience can be forgiven for giving it a dramatic twist. Even those rare governesses who penned their own stories, or who left diaries and letters about their experiences, drew liberally on the resources of fiction and on arguments and images familiar from the 'Governess Question' in the press.

To anyone wishing to venture further into the social history of our subject we recommend Kathryn Hughes's unrivalled study *The Victorian Governess* (1993). Hughes's detailed but engaging account explores the implications of governessing for the relationship between class and gender in the nineteenth century, a theme the reader will recognize in the following chapters. Hughes is concerned to show 'how an understanding of the governess' situation throws light way beyond the door of the Victorian home schoolroom', (pp. xv–xvi). Perhaps because we are both teachers, our own emphasis has been slightly different. We wished to show something of what went on *within* the schoolroom: a subject hitherto rather marginal to histories of the governess. Our first priority has been to discover the governess at work: devising her curriculum, designing and giving lessons, managing – or mismanaging – her pupils, and balancing the many extraneous duties that fell to her lot. Our assumption has been that, though strenuous and often uncomfortable, governessing was not *only* a miserable experience. Charlotte Brontë hated governessing and lost no opportunity to say so. But was this the universal experience? The evidence from textbooks and memoirs offered in this volume suggests that governesses could be imaginative, resourceful, resilient: we even glimpse one playing football. Rather than being simply victims of the Victorian ideal of femininity, governesses helped to forge, perpetuate, and even challenge conventional understandings of what middle-class women could profitably learn, know, and teach.

CHAPTER 1
BECOMING A GOVERNESS

Although the governess had long been a familiar figure in upper-class households, changing economic circumstances in the early part of the nineteenth century meant that the profession became subject to new currents of supply and demand. Money, or the lack of it, largely determined whether or not the daughters of individual families became governesses. For the daughters of merchants, civil servants, navy and military officers and clergymen fallen on hard times, governessing was undoubtedly a step down the social scale; paradoxically, for some daughters of the lower ranks of the rising middle class – farmers and tradesmen, for example – governessing could represent a step up, a means of living among and mingling with those traditionally of higher status. Likewise, employers were no longer exclusively to be found in the ranks of the upper middle class or among the aristocracy; farmers, men of business and factory owners might also hire governesses, who served as much as status symbols for their employer as teachers of their children.

As Pamela Horn (1989) has indicated, the censuses of 1851 and 1861 show a far higher concentration of governesses in London and the Home Counties than in the industrial north of England and in Wales. In the south-east particularly, the new conditions of supply and demand created a complicated, and unregulated, system by which governesses might find a suitable position. In a world of accelerated economic upheaval, procedures for finding work were increasingly impersonal and erratic, and for middle-class women, there was the added problem that the business of actively seeking work at all implied a loss of caste and respectability. To make matters worse, many were forced to go through the mortifying process several times during their careers. Those without friends or relatives who could provide them with an introduction faced the unenviable task of sifting through newspaper advertisements, or contacting employment agencies; others risked censure by taking matters into their own hands and advertising their talents through the pages of the press. Those lucky enough to gain an interview, either in person or (as was often the case) by post, were often subject to highly intrusive questioning about their histories.

On the other hand, market forces favoured employers who, with an ever-burgeoning supply of governesses requiring work, were in the fortunate position of picking and choosing governesses at discount prices. Ironically, though teacher training was largely nonexistent in the early part of the century, employers often demanded an extraordinary array of credentials, both moral and academic, from their governesses. However, the informality of the system also had its pitfalls for employers who, without diplomas or examination results to depend upon, could never be sure of the true educational capabilities of those they employed. Even once the tricky business of applying and appointing had been successfully negotiated, both governess and parents often found that they had got rather more – or less – than they had bargained for when both parties met for the first time.

Given the scramble involved in becoming a governess, it is hardly surprising that advice both to prospective employers and to employees flourished throughout the century, or that numerous accounts of this painful process, tragic and comic, were recorded in contemporary poetry and prose.

THE GOVERNESS CLASSES

In 1847, at the height of what has been characterized as the most difficult period for governesses, Mary Maurice, in a work of advice, wrote of the swift changes of fortune that frequently forced many families to send their daughters out to earn their own living.

And who are these? Multitudes of them are ladies whose tales of sorrow should soften the hearts of those, who in looking upon their own offspring, can never tell that they may not hereafter be also exiled from their happy homes. Many were the children of affluent parents, who brought them up with every indulgence and refinement, that wealth could bestow: they moved in the best circles, and expected that their prosperity would last for ever; but a sudden loss of fortune, a failure in business, or death, has reversed the picture, and no alternative remains, but that they must support themselves, and no other way but this is open to them. Many were the daughters of clergymen, who were courted and followed; their houses were the resort of the wealthy members of their congregations; but their incomes were limited, and they had only a life-interest in them, and these were wholly swallowed up, in necessary expenses and in educating their children. The latter naturally acquired the tastes and feelings of the society with which they associated, and they were not unfrequently flattered too, till they fancied themselves the objects of admiration, instead of perceiving, that they were only sought after, as the ready means of access, to the popular preacher. But the father sickens, and dies, the orphaned family are at once reduced to want; the girls must find homes for themselves; perhaps the majority being only half educated, must be kept at school, by the scanty earnings of their elder sisters, till they too can find means of support.

Again, let us picture to ourselves the family of a country clergyman, which has been carefully brought up under the eye of a tender mother. The children are growing up happy members of

Fig. 4 The lonely, homesick governess was a familiar feature of Victorian iconography.

a peaceful home, where all the charities of life are in full exercise, where each heart is bound to each, by the holiest bonds, and the parents live for them, for each other, and for God. They are trained by the constant exercise of self-denial, to do good to the parish in which they dwell, and they shed a living light, the reflection of the truths their father teaches. Their house is one of the beautiful country parsonages, which so sweetly adorn our land, and give at once the idea of peace and repose; but the circle rapidly increasing, the utmost economy will not suffice to meet the growing expenditure; sickness enters the dwelling, and at length it becomes painfully evident, that the elder daughters must enter upon the life of governesses, and that they may save the rest from ruin, they quit the spot so much endeared to them – sisters who have never been separated before, must go out into the cold world, their only comfort being, that hereafter

> They shall meet, no wanderer lost,
> A family in heaven.

It was from a member of such a circle that we can fancy the well-known picture was taken of 'the New Governess'. The poor girl is sitting dressed in mourning, with an open letter in her hand, and the young children near her idling over their books, whilst the elder girls are amusing themselves in another part of the room.

[. . .]

Another large class of governesses is formed from the daughters of officers in the army or navy; men who filled during their lives high positions, but at their death nothing remained for the support of their children, but a small pension, and that granted only during their minority. Many of these young persons are nearly connected with the nobility, and have often, in their dependent position, to struggle with all the pride of birth and blood, the sense of the miserable change that has come over them, and the consciousness that but for the power which mere wealth confers, they are greatly superior to their employers, and pupils, both in education, and rank.

[Mary Maurice], *Mothers and Governesses* (1847), pp. 18–21.

STRUGGLING UP OR DRIFTING DOWN

It was the ambiguous social origin of the governess that made her such an enigmatic figure. An anonymous article in the first edition of The English Woman's Journal *(1858) commented that the profession of governessing, with its broad intake, actually elided distinctions of rank between women.*

Indeed, it is not a question of rank at all, for the unmarried members of the small merchant's family enter the profession from natural necessity, and the fortuneless daughters of the highly connected clergyman have often no other resource. It is a platform on which middle and upper classes meet, the one struggling up, the other drifting down. If a father dies, or a bank breaks, or a husband is killed, – if brothers require a college education to fit them for one of the many careers open to an M.A., or orphan nephews and nieces are cast helpless upon a woman's heart, here is the one means of breadwinning to which access alone seems open, – to which alone untrained capacity is equal or pride admits appeal.

[Bessie Rayner Parkes], 'The Profession of the Teacher' (1858), p. 1.

A NEW SERVITUDE

For those who 'struggled up', the prospect of governessing might represent an escape from other hardships. To Jane Eyre, after eight years at Lowood School, the possibility of obtaining a position as governess in a private household appeared as an opportunity (albeit a modest one) for applying talents, exercising independence, and acquiring new experiences and new friends.

'A new servitude! There is something in that,' I soliloquized (mentally, be it understood; I did not talk aloud). 'I know there is, because it does not sound too sweet; it is not like such words as Liberty, Excitement, Enjoyment: delightful sounds truly, but no more than sounds for me, and so hollow and fleeting that it is mere waste of time to listen to them. But Servitude! That must be a matter of fact. Any one may serve: I have served here eight years; now all I want is to serve elsewhere. Can I not get so much of my own will! Is not the thing feasible! Yes – yes – the end is not so difficult, if I had only a brain active enough to ferret out the means of attaining it.'

I sat up in bed by way of arousing this said brain. It was a chilly night; I covered my shoulders with a shawl, and then I proceeded to *think* again with all my might.

'What do I want? A new place, in a new house, amongst new faces, under new circumstances. I want this because it is of no use wanting anything better. How do people do to get a new place? They apply to friends, I suppose. I have no friends. There are many others who have no friends, who must look about for themselves and be their own helpers; and what is their resource?'

Charlotte Brontë, *Jane Eyre* (1847, reprinted 1985), pp. 117–18.

A FEW PLAIN CREDENTIALS

Jane Eyre was fortunate in so far as her role as teacher to the younger pupils at Lowood had made her well qualified for the task of governessing. In fact few of those women who became governesses in the early part of the century had enjoyed any formal education in the art of teaching. This state of affairs, however, seemed to have little effect on the demands made by employers. In a buyer's market they could ask for the highest accomplishments. From the early 1830s onwards, the exorbitant demands of employers and their contradictory expectations were a common butt of satire. In this poem by Maria Abdy, a sister asks her brother to take note of her requirements for a new governess.

A Governess Wanted

'Our governess left us, dear brother,
Last night, in a strange fit of pique,
Will you kindly seek out for another?
We want her at latest next week:

19

But I'll give you a few plain credentials,
The bargain with speed to complete;
Take a pen – just set down the essentials,
And begin at the top of the sheet!

'With easy and modest decision,
She ever must move, act, and speak;
She must understand French with precision,
Italian, and Latin, and Greek:
She must play the piano divinely,
Excel on the harp and the lute,
Do all sorts of needle-work finely,
And make feather-flowers, and wax-fruit.

'She must answer all queries directly,
And all sciences well understand,
Paint in oils, sketch from nature correctly,
And write German text, and short-hand:
She must sing with power, science, and sweetness,
Yet for concerts must sigh not at all,
She must dance with etherial fleetness;
Yet never must go to a ball.

'She must not have needy relations,
Her dress must be tasteful yet plain,
Her discourse must abound in quotations,
Her memory all dates must retain:
She must point out each author's chief beauties,
She must manage dull natures with skill,
Her pleasures must lie in her duties,
She must never be nervous or ill!

'If she write essays, odes, themes, and sonnets,
Yet be not pedantic or pert;
If she wear none but deep cottage bonnets,
If she deem it high treason to flirt,

If to mildness she add sense and spirit,
Engage her at once without fear;
I love to reward modest merit,
And I give – forty guineas a year.'

'I accept, my good sister, your mission,
To-morrow, my search I'll begin –
In all circles, in every condition,
I'll strive such a treasure to win;
And, if after years of probation,
My eyes on the wonder should rest,
I'll engage her without hesitation,
But not on the terms you suggest.

'Of a bride I have ne'er made selection,
For my bachelor thoughts would still dwell
On an object so near to perfection,
That I blushed half my fancies to tell;
Now this list that you kindly have granted,
I'll quote and refer to through life,
But just blot out – "A Governess Wanted",
And head it with – "Wanted a Wife!"'

Maria Abdy, *Poetry* (1838), pp. 21–3.

A BUYER'S MARKET

*Once she had replied to an advert, the prospective governess steeled
herself for any response from outright rejection to an invitation to
interview. While many governesses were prepared to move large
distances in order to obtain suitable employment, it was
impracticable to expect women to travel up and down the country
for interview. Employers sometimes devised ingenious methods by
which to sift out unsuitable applicants. Questionnaires like the one
below, copied in anger to* The Times *in 1849, were not always*

welcomed by their recipients. By 1850 such bothersome interrogation was considered, by some members of the reading public at least, to be intrusive, if not outrageous.

Wanted a Governess

The following reply was sent some time since to an application by a lady for the situation of a governess: the salary offered was 30*l*.:–

It is requested that the following questions be answered by letter: they are intended to prevent unnecessary trouble; the answer will be considered strictly confidential:–

1. Please to give your name and address.
2. What is your age?
3. Have you any matrimonial engagement?
4. State the name and address of the family in which you were last engaged as governess.
5. How many pupils had you? Were they girls or boys, and what were their ages?
6. How long were you there, and how long is it since you left?
7. Did you instruct without the aid of masters? If not, state what masters assisted.
8. Similar particulars with respect to the former situations which you have held.
9. Please to give the address of your parents, and state their occupation.
10. State the names, addresses, and occupations of any other of your near relations, or intimate friends.
11. Where were you educated, and was your education conducted with reference to your present occupation as a governess?
12. Have you a good knowledge of English grammar and geography?
13. Are you conversant with the histories of England, Greece, and Rome, and with sacred history?
14. Have you a knowledge of the elements of either of the following sciences – botany, astronomy, natural philosophy, natural history, chymistry?

15. With which of the religious, or moral authors, or poets, are you familiar, and with which of the historians, or authors in polite literature, are you acquainted?
16. Do you speak the French language fluently?
17. Did you acquire it on the continent?

[. . .]

'Wanted a Governess', *The Times* (16 April 1849), p. 8.

STRIKING A BARGAIN

Governesses did not, as is sometimes implied, automatically accept the poor conditions offered by uncharitable employers. Many advertised their own services through the columns of newspapers and more specialized magazines, and though these adverts are reminders of the degradation and desperation to which some had sunk, they do indicate a degree of independence among governesses in their demand for fairer terms and, perhaps, a recognition of the need for self-protection in an exploitative marketplace. Anne Brontë, no doubt harking back to her own painful experiences as a governess with the Ingham family at Blake Hall (1839) and with the Robinson family at Thorp Green Hall (1841–45), allowed her fictional heroine Agnes Grey a degree of autonomy in the process of selecting her second situation.

. . . I searched, with great interest, the advertising columns of the newspapers, and wrote answers to every 'Wanted a Governess,' that appeared at all eligible; but all my letters, as well as the replies, when I got any, were dutifully shewn to my mother; and she, to my chagrin, made me reject the situations one after another – These were low people, these were too exacting in their demands, and these too niggardly in their remunerations.

'Your talents are not such as every poor clergyman's daughter possesses, Agnes,' she would say, 'and you must not throw them away. Remember, you promised to be patient – there is no need of hurry – you have plenty of time before you, and may have many chances yet.'

At length she advised me to put an advertisement, myself, in the paper, stating my qualifications, &c.

'Music, Singing, Drawing, French, Latin, and German,' said she, 'are no mean assemblage; many will be glad to have so much in one instructor; and this time, you shall try your fortune in a somewhat higher family – in that of some genuine, thorough-bred gentleman, for such are far more likely to treat you with proper respect and consideration, than those purse-proud trades-people, and arrogant upstarts. I have known several among higher ranks, who treated their governess quite as one of the family; though some, I allow, are as insolent and exacting as any one else can be; for there are bad and good in all classes.'

The advertisement was quickly written and despatched. Of the two parties who answered it, but one would consent to give me fifty pounds, the sum my mother bade me name as the salary I should require; and here, I hesitated about engaging myself, as I feared the children would be too old, and their parents would require some one more showy, or more experienced, if not more accomplished than I; but my mother dissuaded me from declining it on that account: I should do vastly well, she said, if I would only throw aside my diffidence, and acquire a little more confidence in myself. I was just to give a plain, true, statement of my acquirements and qualifications, and name what stipulations I chose to make, and then await the result.

The only stipulation I ventured to propose, was that I might be allowed two months' holidays during the year to visit my friends, at Midsummer and Christmas. The unknown lady, in her reply, made no objection to this, and stated that, as to my acquirements, she had no doubt that I should be able to give satisfaction; but in the engagement of governesses, she considered those things as subordinate points, as, being situated in the neighbourhood of O—, she could get masters to supply any deficiencies in that respect, but, in her opinion, next to unimpeachable morality, a mild and cheerful temper and obliging disposition were the most essential requisites.

My mother did not relish this at all, and now made many objections to my accepting the situation, in which my sister warmly supported her;

but, unwilling to be baulked again, I overruled them all; and, having first obtained the consent of my father, who had, a short time previously, been apprised of these transactions, I wrote a most obliging epistle to my unknown correspondent, and, finally, the bargain was concluded.

It was decreed that, on the last day of January, I was to enter upon my new office, as governess in the family of Mr Murray, of Harden Lodge, near O—, about seventy miles from our village – a formidable distance to me, as I had never been above twenty miles from home in all the course of my twenty years sojourn on earth, and as, moreover, every individual, in that family and in the neighbourhood, was utterly unknown to myself and all my acquaintances.

Anne Brontë, *Agnes Grey* (1848, reprinted 1988), pp. 56–8.

AN INTRODUCTION THROUGH FRIENDS

Placing adverts and applying to agencies for a position were perhaps the most humiliating, because the most public, part of the whole business of becoming a governess. In a classic scene from Jane Austen's Emma *(1816), the respectable and financially stable world of Highbury is temporarily disturbed by the news that the accomplished Jane Fairfax may soon need to earn her living as a teacher in the homes of others. However out of sympathy with the snobbish and overbearing Mrs Elton in her repeated and ingratiating offers of help, the reader can only share her horror at Jane's idea of going to an 'agency'. Jane's startling equation of governessing with the slave trade is an unsettling reminder of the terrors life could hold for those single women of the period less fortunate than the refined Emma Woodhouse herself.*

The post-office – catching cold – fetching letters – and friendship, were long under discussion; and to them succeeded one, which must be at least equally unpleasant to Jane – inquiries whether she had yet heard of any situation likely to suit her, and professions of Mrs Elton's meditated activity.

'Here is April come!' said she, 'I get quite anxious about you. June will soon be here.'

'But I have never fixed on June or any other month – merely looked forward to the summer in general.'

'But have you really heard of nothing?

'I have not even made any inquiry; I do not wish to make any yet.'

'Oh! my dear, we cannot begin too early; you are not aware of the difficulty of procuring exactly the desirable thing.'

'I, not aware!' said Jane, shaking her head; 'dear Mrs Elton, who can have thought of it as I have done?'

'But you have not seen so much of the world as I have. You do not know how many candidates there always are for the *first* situations. I saw a vast deal of that in the neighbourhood round Maple Grove. A cousin of Mr Suckling, Mrs Bragge, had such an infinity of applications; every body was anxious to be in her family, for she moves in the first circle. Wax-candles in the schoolroom! You may imagine how desirable! Of all houses in the kingdom, Mrs Bragge's is the one I would most wish to see you in.'

'Col. and Mrs Campbell are to be in town again by mid-summer,' said Jane. 'I must spend some time with them; I am sure they will want it; – afterwards I may probably be glad to dispose of myself. But I would not wish you to take the trouble of making any inquiries at present.'

'Trouble! aye, I know your scruples. You are afraid of giving me trouble; but I assure you, my dear Jane, the Campbells can hardly be more interested about you than I am. I shall write to Mrs Partridge in a day or two, and shall give her a strict charge to be on the look-out for anything eligible.'

'Thank you but I would rather you did not mention the subject to her; till the time draws nearer, I do not wish to be giving any body trouble.'

'But my dear child, the time *is* drawing near, here is April, and June, or say even July, is very near, with such business to accomplish before us. Your inexperience really amuses me! A situation such as you deserve, and your friends would require for you, is no every day occurrence, is not obtained at a moment's notice; indeed, indeed, we must begin inquiring directly.'

'Excuse me, ma'am, but this is by no means my intention; I make no inquiry myself, and should be sorry to have any made by my friends. When I am quite determined as to the time, I am not at all afraid of being long unemployed. There are places in town, offices, where inquiry would soon produce something – Offices for the sale – not quite of human flesh – but of human intellect.'

'Oh! my dear, human flesh! You quite shock me: if you mean a fling at the slave trade, I assure you Mr Suckling was always rather a friend to the abolition.'

'I did not mean, I was not thinking of the slave-trade,' replied Jane; 'governess-trade, I assure you, was all that I had in view; widely different certainly as to the guilt of those who carry it on; but as to the greater misery of the victims, I do not know where it lies. But I only mean to say that there are advertising offices, and that by applying to them I should have no doubt of very soon meeting with something that would do.'

'Something that would do!' repeated Mrs Elton. 'Aye, *that* may suit your humble ideas of yourself; – I know what a modest creature you are; but it will not satisfy your friends to have you taking up with any thing that may offer, any inferior, common-place situation, in a family not moving in a certain circle, or able to command the elegancies of life.'

'You are very obliging; but as to all that, I am very indifferent; it would be no object to me to be with the rich; my mortifications, I think, would only be the greater; I should suffer more from comparison. A gentleman's family is all I should condition for.'

'I know you, I know you; you would take up with any thing; but I shall be a little more nice, and I am sure the good Campbells will be quite on my side; with your superior talents, you have a right to move in the first circle. Your musical knowledge alone would entitle you to name your own terms, have as many rooms as you like, and mix in the family as much as you chose; – and you must and shall be delightfully, honourably and comfortably settled before the Campbells or I have any rest.'

'You may well class the delight, the honour, and the comfort of such a situation together,' said Jane, 'they are pretty sure to be equal; however, I am very serious in not wishing any thing to be attempted at present for me. I am exceedingly obliged to you, Mrs Elton, I am obliged to any body who feels for me, but I am quite serious in wishing nothing to be done till the summer. For two or three months longer I shall remain where I am, and as I am.'

'And I am quite serious too, I assure you,' replied Mrs Elton gaily, 'in resolving to be always on the watch, and employing my friends to watch also, that nothing really unexceptionable may pass us.'

Jane Austen, *Emma* (1816, reprinted 1977), pp. 299–301.

YOU MUST BE PATIENT

Writers of guidance for governesses made much of the trials involved in applying for a position. In 1869, Emily Peart reminded her readers to be sanguine about rejections, to be reasonable in their own expectations and, above all, to keep trying.

After questionings, and doubts, and anxieties, you come to the determination to teach, and you inquire after a situation; and here, again, you must be patient. You may have long to wait; you may have hopes of many situations, and be disappointed; you may miss one you think would have suited you, and you may at last be compelled to accept one which is not at all what you would wish; but if it comes immediately before you, in the plain path of duty; only be sure it is the plain path of duty, take it; only be sure it *is* the plain path of duty, or you cannot enter it rightly. It is very trying for some ladies to receive into their houses those whom they feel to be in a reduced position; and they naturally prefer ladies who have been educated for the work of teaching, and who have all along kept this in view. There are strong objections in the minds of some, to a lady who is compelled unexpectedly to teach, and to teach just for a living. You will find this a great obstacle to a good situation. Few would willingly receive into their homes one who is in great trouble; few especially would choose such a one as an instructress for their children, who need, and *must have*, a cheerful, sympathizing person with them.

[. . .]

Expect, then, again and again to miss an opportunity, and not to obtain a situation about which you are asking. If you are in treaty for a situation, if it be possible make salary scarcely any object. You cannot command a large one, because you have had no experience. Respectability and character in those with whom you are going to reside are the chief things; make sure of these – as sure as it is possible to be, and let salary at first be quite a minor consideration. On your first situation, and what it is to you, and you to it, depend mainly the comfort and success of your future career. On no account let a higher salary influence you if other requirements are questionable; it is nothing to you *now* compared with the integrity and uprightness of your employers.

[Emily Peart], *A Book for Governesses* (1869), pp. 17–19.

A POSTING TO BAGHDAD

For important positions, governesses could be interviewed, either by the family itself, or if it lived abroad, by a panel of interested parties acting on the family's behalf. In this fictionalized account of the appointment of a young girl, Cecil Ansthruther, as governess to Azim Shams-ed-Din Bey, son and heir to his Excellency the Emperor of Baghdad, Hilda Caroline Gregg (using the pseudonym Sydney Grier) dramatizes just how daunting such interviews could be. Chapter 5 will explore the adventures of the governess abroad. For now, it is worth noting how Grier, who wrote frequently on Eastern themes, assumes that the supposedly upright moral demeanour of the English governess, and by implication her Englishness itself, are as important recommendations for employment overseas as the testimonials to her academic competence.

There were some eight or nine gentlemen present, the chief of whom seemed to be a grey-haired man at the end of the table. His face was in some way familiar to Cecil, but it was not at first that she remembered she had seen him in close attendance on the Turkish ambassador on his way to some State function. Next to him, on either side, sat Lady Haigh and Denarien Bey, and then came several vivacious, dark-eyed gentlemen in fezzes, who talked among themselves with a great deal of gesticulation, and seemed to bear a kind of national likeness to the Armenian envoy. Somewhat apart from the rest sat a stout elderly Englishman, with a stolid and unconvinced expression, and a general air of being present to keep other people from being imposed upon. There was also a secretary – a slim dark-skinned youth in spectacles, who scribbled notes in a large clasped book, when he was not nibbling his pen and staring at Cecil; and lastly, at the very end of the table, Cecil and Miss Arbuthnot themselves. Cecil was in a hopeless state of amazement and mystification, feeling, moreover, a terrible inclination to giggle on finding herself the cynosure of all the eyes in the room. What could it all mean? Was it possible that Ahmed Khémi Pasha, who was said to be fond of European innovations, was going to found a High School in Baghdad? and was she to take charge of it? But no; Miss Arbuthnot had said that the situation was to be in a private family. What could be going to happen?

There was a little low-toned conversation between the two gentlemen at the head of the table, and then Denarien Bey spoke.

'We have heard, mademoiselle, that you are willing to accept a situation as governess out of England – a course seldom adopted by young ladies of your high attainments. This suggested to her ladyship,' he bowed to Lady Haigh, 'and myself the idea that you might be found the proper person to undertake a charge of a very delicate and important nature. Before saying more, I must impress upon you that all that passes here is in strict confidence, whether the result of this interview is satisfactory or the reverse.'

Cecil bowed, and he went on –

'I think I shall hardly be committing an indiscretion if I mention in the present company that his Excellency Ahmed Khémi Pasha, whom I have the honour to represent here, intends to make his third son, Azim Shams-ed-Din Bey, his heir. A cause may be found for this in the unsatisfactory character of his Excellency's eldest son; and there are also other family reasons which render it imperative. His Excellency has always felt a profound admiration for the English people, and this has of late so much increased that he is anxious to secure an English governess for the Bey, who is now about ten years old. As I was about to visit England, his Excellency thought it fit to confide to me the duty of finding a lady with suitable qualifications who would be willing to accept the post, and I, feeling the charge too heavy for me, even with the kind and experienced help of her ladyship, have taken the precaution of associating with myself my good friend Tussûn Bey,' here he bowed to the old gentleman at the head of the table, 'and these other kind friends.'

There was another interlude of bowing, and Denarien Bey continued –

'The special qualifications which his Excellency desired me to seek in the lady who is to have the charge of his sons are these: she must be capable of carrying on and completing the Bey's education in all but strictly military subjects; and she must be young and – and – well, not disagreeable-looking, that the Bey may feel inclined to learn from her; she must be discreet and not given to making mischief; and she must have been trained in the best methods of teaching. May I trouble you, mademoiselle, to bring your testimonials to this end of the table?'

Somewhat surprised, Cecil rose and carried her bundle of papers to him, while the other gentlemen all turned round on their chairs to look at her, apparently to ascertain whether she fulfilled the second condition satisfactorily.

'I think, gentlemen,' said Tussûn Bey in French, 'that if Mademoiselle Antaza' – he made a bold attempt at the unmanageable name – 'finds herself able to accept the situation, his Excellency will be much gratified by her appearance. She is thoroughly English.'

31

'*Vraiment anglaise!*' ran down the table as all the gentlemen gazed critically at the tall slight figure in the severely simple tweed dress and cloth jacket, with the small close hat and short veil crowning the smooth hair. Cecil returned blushing to her place, while Denarien Bey explained to his assessors the purport of the various testimonials; and the secretary, finding Miss Arbuthnot's eye upon him, made copious notes. After a time the papers were all returned to Denarien Bey, the gentlemen making remarks on them in two or three strange-sounding dialects; and after receiving a paper from the secretary, the Pasha's representative proceeded to explain the terms which were offered.

The salary proposed was a large one, but the Pasha was anxious that his son's course of study should be uninterrupted, and it was therefore his endeavour to secure for it an unbroken period of five years by the following plan. Cecil was to sign an agreement, if her services were engaged, to serve for two years, and on the expiration of this term she could, if she was willing, at once sign another bond to remain three years more, after which she was to be entitled to a large extra bonus in consideration of her labours in conducting Azim Bey's education to a successful close. If Cecil broke the agreement, she was to forfeit the salary for all but the time she had actually served; but if it was broken by the Pasha for any cause excepting her misconduct, the balance was to be paid to her. By the end of the five years Azim Bey would be fifteen, and old enough to be emancipated from female control, and Cecil might return to her own country after an uninterrupted absence of five years.

Cecil's heart sank as she listened. When she heard the amount of salary offered, she had eagerly calculated what she could do for the boys with it, and the mention of the bonus raised high hopes in her heart, until she realised the conditions under which alone it was to be gained. Actually to expatriate herself for five whole years! Never to see England, or her father, or cheerful little Mrs Anstruther, or any of those dear dreadful children for five years! It was too appalling.

Sydney C. Grier, *His Excellency's English Governess* (1896), pp. 19–23.

ADVICE TO A YOUNG GOVERNESS

*Having obtained a position, many young governesses were rightly
anxious about their lack of experience and training. To assuage
such apprehension, advice writers, some of them former
governesses themselves, warmed to the task of preparing younger
women for the trials ahead. In and among the inevitable platitudes
and generalizations, there were often nuggets of genuine wisdom
and invaluable guidance on practical matters.*

When I first, some sixteen years ago, was introduced to a school-room, with four dear children, whom I was to teach as I thought best, I should have been not only interested, but helped, by such suggestions as I mean to take courage now to put down. The subject is boundless; all is not said that there is to say; and, though there are many speakers and writers at whose feet I would gladly sit to learn from them, yet, perhaps the very simplicity of what is in my mind to write, may leave me a place to fill up still unoccupied by them.

I imagine you, then, (and I am sure I feel a hearty sympathy with you,) entering on your new post, with a strong feeling of interest in the plans you are about to form, and with sufficient liveliness of mind not to be content with shaping them, as the first resource that occurs to you, after the pattern of the school you have yourself just left.

I am not going to write a treatise on education. I have not ability for that. My aim is, only, to say a few simple things to a person in the condition in which I recollect myself to have been.

First. Ask of God to give you the mind that was in Christ. So to fill your heart with His love, that your whole spirit and manner may breathe the sweetness of it, and that you may be honoured to win your dear pupils to the Cross. To give you special patience and good temper, for you may be sure you will have special need of them; and, besides this, graciously to bless your endeavours to acquire that without which you cannot be successful, and which may be made matter of acquirement – something of that happy manner by which we bring our influence to bear on our fellow creatures without *friction*.

Then, go and buy Isaac Taylor's 'Home Education', and Abbott's 'Teacher'. Do not read them and put them away, but have them always at hand. Talk to successful teachers, ask them questions, no matter how simple, about their management. *You will always find the most successful ready to acknowledge that they themselves are always learning*, and that, too, sometimes by their own mistakes. But do not copy the plans, or receive the counsel of any, whose pupils are not *happy*, as well as intelligent.

Gain access to all the school-rooms you can; good or bad, you will learn from them all; you will see, in all their varieties, the manners to be cultivated, and the manners to be avoided. [. . .] You must notice teachers who are obeyed as you wish to be obeyed; loved, as you wish to be loved. Some morning, when the spirit of your school-room has been, to an unusual degree, of that serenely cheerful nature most favourable both to moral and intellectual progress, consider what part *you* have had in producing it, and how you can best promote it in future. And when it is otherwise, go as soon as you can, and walk out in the fresh air; and when your head has done aching (not before, or you will see all things through a yellow glass), recall the state in which *you* began the morning's work. Were you well? and cheerful? and ready to see everything in the pleasantest light in which it could truthfully be seen?

The next thing we would say to you is, *Give up entirely the expectation that you will ever see your pupils perfect*. If you are too eager; if (to use a phrase more expressive than refined) you are always *at* them about one thing or another; if, whilst they are rewarding the pains you take to interest them by the glowing looks with which they listen to you, you break off, and throw a damp on the whole, by stopping to correct some unfortunate elbow which is, probably, just in the position which an artist would choose for it, and in which papa and mamma sit every day; then, farewell to your success. This exercise of authority about every trifle, 'is like shooting butterflies with cannon-balls' as one said to me, whose views of education Pestalozzi declared, of all he had met with in England, most nearly to reach his ideal. If you will bring out your cannon continually, you must be content with butterflies. When an important occasion arises, you cannot meet it, for you have nothing heavier than what you have used before.

[. . .]

I was only a few years old, in my own teaching career, when I heard the observation made, with reference to a particular school, 'And they get as much as possible out of the boys, I suppose?' 'Before they do that,' was the reply, 'they *put what they can into them.*' This remark has often occurred to me, as illustrative of the natural order to be observed in the processes of education. The business of its first years should be, mainly, *putting in*; communicating facts, of which abundance exists, adapted to enrich the mind, without fatiguing it. Many things in which we instruct our children have their chief value simply in this way; viz., by giving their minds, which are sure to work upon something, something interesting and sensible on which to work. . . . Your young ladies will not be likely ever to have practical need for showing that 'all the angles of a triangle are equal to two right angles;' yet it is not possible they can study the proposition, provided they do so with pleasure, without being improved by it.

Anon., *A Word to a Young Governess by an Old One* (1860), pp. 3–9.

AN INDULGENT EMPLOYER

Of course, no amount of good advice could prepare the new governess sufficiently for her first day at work. Mary Cowden-Clarke, daughter of the composer Vincent Novello, had been sent in the late 1820s to Boulogne to learn French as a prelude to her future career as a governess. But her record of her first working day, described in her memoir of 1896, reminds us that a rapport with one's employer was perhaps a more important guarantee of success than qualifications.

Fig. 5 George Goodwin Kilburne's *The Introduction* hints at the awkwardness of a
governess's first moments with her new pupils.

On my return to England, it was agreed that I should begin my intended
profession – that of a governess; and an engagement was soon found
for me in the family of a gentleman and lady named Purcell, four of whose
children I was to teach. The 'four' proved really to be five, for the youngest
was oftener sent to the schoolroom than kept in the nursery. However,
nothing could be kinder to me than the lady of the house. I was taken
down, late one evening, in their chariot to their country residence at
Cranford, and it was a curious experience to find myself seated in the dark,
with perfect strangers beside me, being driven to a spot I had never seen.
But when I saw it next morning I found it a most attractive 'cottage orné'.

Its groundfloor rooms were fitted up in the tastefullest style, one with a trellised papering of honeysuckles, interspersed with mirrors let into the wall; another with roses, chandeliers, girandoles, and so on, that took my girlish fancy immensely. Before seeing this pretty interior I had been into the garden, for I was always an early riser; and, moreover, I wanted a quiet hour to make myself acquainted with my new surroundings, and also to look over the lessons I should have to give my young pupils during the day. Even thus immediately I experienced the kindness of my lady-employer; for when she learned that I had asked whether I might eat an apple that I found fallen on the grass, she gave me leave to take an apple from the tree whenever I felt inclined to eat one before breakfast.

Mary Cowden-Clarke, *My Long Life* (1896), pp. 31–2.

NIL DESPERANDUM

Surprises were as often in store for employers as for governesses themselves. After the death of her husband in Singapore in 1858, Welsh-born Anna Harriette Leonowens tried to support herself and her family by opening a school for officers' children. In 1862 Anna's reputation as a teacher reached the ears of the king of Siam, who summoned her to instruct his prodigious family. In this classic account of her arrival as governess to the children of the Siamese court, the authoritarian king is bemused by the wit and audacity of his hireling at their first meeting.

In the Oriental tongues this progressive king was eminently proficient; and toward priests, preachers, and teachers, of all creeds, sects, and sciences, an enlightened exemplar of tolerance. It was likewise his peculiar vanity to pass for an accomplished English scholar, and to this end he maintained in his palace at Bangkok a private printing establishment, with fonts of English type, which, as may be perceived presently, he was at no loss to keep in 'copy'. Perhaps it was the printing-office which suggested, quite naturally, an English governess for the *élite* of his wives and concubines, and their offspring, – in number amply adequate to the constitution of a royal school, and in material most attractively fresh and romantic. Happy thought! Wherefore, behold me, just after sunset on a pleasant day in April 1862, on the threshold of the outer court of the Grand Palace, accompanied by my own brave little boy, and escorted by a compatriot.

A flood of light sweeping through the spacious Hall of Audience displayed a throng of noblemen in waiting. None turned a glance, or seemingly a thought, on us, and, my child being tired and hungry, I urged Captain B— to present us without delay. At once we mounted the marble steps, and entered the brilliant hall unannounced. Ranged on the carpet were many prostrate, mute, and motionless forms, over whose heads to step was a temptation as drolly natural as it was dangerous. His Majesty spied us quickly, and advanced abruptly, petulantly screaming, 'Who? who? who?'

Captain B— (who, by the by, is a titled nobleman of Siam) introduced me as the English governess, engaged for the royal family. The king shook hands with us, and immediately proceeded to march up and down in quick step, putting one foot before the other with mathematical precision, as if under drill. [. . .] Suddenly his Majesty, having cogitated sufficiently in his peculiar manner, with one long final stride halted in front of us, and, pointing straight at me with his forefinger, asked, 'How old shall you be?'

Scarcely able to repress a smile at a proceeding so absurd, and with my sex's distaste for so serious a question, I demurely replied, 'One hundred and fifty years old.'

Had I made myself much younger, he might have ridiculed or assailed me; but now he stood surprised and embarrassed for a few moments, then resumed his queer march; and at last, beginning to perceive the jest, coughed, laughed, coughed again, and in a high, sharp key asked, 'In what year were you borncd?'

Instantly I struck a mental balance, and answered, as gravely as I could, 'In 1788.' At this point the expression of his Majesty's face was indescribably comical. Captain B— slipped behind a pillar to laugh; but the king only coughed, with a significant emphasis that startled me, and addressed a few words to his prostrate courtiers, who smiled at the carpet, – all except the prime minister, who turned to look at me. But his Majesty was not to be baffled so: again he marched with vigor, and then returned to the attack with *élan*.

'How many years shall you be married?'

'For several years, your Majesty.'

[. . .]

'I have sixty-seven children,' said his Majesty, when we had returned to the Audience Hall. 'You shall educate them, and as many of my wives, likewise, as may wish to learn English. And I have much correspondence in which you must assist me. And, moreover, I have much difficulty for reading and translating French letters; for French are fond of using gloomily deceiving terms. You must undertake; and you shall make all their murky sentences and gloomily deceiving propositions clear to me. And, furthermore, I have by every mail foreign letters whose writing is not easily read by me. You shall copy on round hand, for my readily perusal thereof.'

Nil desperandum; but I began by despairing of my ability to accomplish tasks so multifarious. I simply bowed, however, and so dismissed myself for that evening.

Anna Harriette Leonowens, *The English Governess at the Siamese Court* (1870), pp. 56–9.

CHAPTER 2

A WORKING LIFE

For the governess, the first week in her new household was often a trial of academic competence, social skills and endurance.

W. Rothery's Esqre,
18 James St.
Buckingham Palace.

Y ou must know, my dear Mother, that I wrote you a very long letter last night giving you a full description of my new home & prospects, & this morning, when we went for our usual walk, Harriett (my little pupil) was very desirous of keeping them in her bag until we came to the Post Office. I accordingly saw them safely deposited in her bag, &, lo, when she came to put them in the letter box we found one was missing & that happened to be yours. We came back directly but could not see anything of the lost letter. I hope some well-disposed person will chance to find it & then instead of being opened & read it will be posted & you [will] get it quite safe. This has worried me very much. I hate anything of the kind. I then wrote a hasty line or two in pencil that you might not be uncomfortable which I suppose you have received all safe.

We do not regularly begin study until next Wednesday & as yet I have merely been questioning my little girl to ascertain what she really knows. I find she is rather advanced for her age, being only 9. She reads & understands French very well, knows a little Latin, & plays pretty well – indeed I never had a music pupil who played so steadily or had so few bad habits to correct (of course I mean for her age) and am delighted to have a pupil who has been so well *grounded* in music; of course this gives one an additional interest in teaching her. She is tractable but from being the only girl has been a little indulged, I fancy, but not to make her disagreeable. She is a perfect child in mind and manners, so that I cannot communicate a single thought or feeling in which she could share, & then for a little while I feel it miserably, wretchedly dull.

My study is at the back of the house, so nothing is to be seen from that. My bedroom [is a] larger room in the front overlooking the front of the Palace & the Barracks, & were it not that I see constantly *living* beings *really* moving backwards & forwards there I should fancy I was to be shut up here for ever without knowing any one who could enter into one's feelings.

The wind is howling a good deal tonight & I think of my darling brother much & of the beloved lost one. I feel I shall get very melancholy here. I know not what it may be in summer. However, here it has pleased God to place me and I must make the best of it I can. Be sure you write & tell me where to find you on Xmas day. I hope you are going with me.

I am afraid Miss Morgan is vexed that I did not take the situation at Stratford on Avon. I certainly should have seen a little society there.

My kind remembrances to all in Broad Street. Goodbye, dear Mother,

Ever your affecte. Child,
Elizth.

Friday Even.__

I was reading a few minutes since and met with some lines by Coleridge which are certainly very appropriate to me just now –

> And I have not a common hope with any,
> Thus, like one drop of oil upon a flood,
> In uncommunicating solitude
> Alone I am amid –

A.H. Chisholm, *Elizabeth Gould, Some 'New' Letters* (written *c.* 1827, published 1964), pp. 321–6.

As this poignant letter home records, the first task of the new governess was to meet and assess her pupils. Much depended on their number. Elizabeth was perhaps fortunate in her single pupil. Ellen Weeton, a Lancashire governess and keeper of journals, found herself dealing with six children when she resided with the Armitage family in Yorkshire; and numbers could increase as younger children left the nursery for the schoolroom. Devising a timetable which would simultaneously suit the needs of children of various ages required organizational dexterity and flexibility. Moreover, until her male pupils left for private schools, usually at the ages of about twelve or thirteen, the governess would be responsible for the education of children of both sexes. In a system in which gender differentiation was important, the governess faced the challenge of inventing a curriculum that would benefit all her pupils.

In addition, the governess was often required to deal with children who had already passed through the hands of several governesses. Lucy Lyttleton's diaries for the 1840s and 1850s record a steady stream of governesses (Miss Nicholson, Miss Crump, Miss Pearson, a stout French governess, Miss Smith . . .), ranging from the stern to the lenient (cited in Horn, 1997, p. 43). Such a rapid turnover was no doubt unsettling for the children, who had to adapt to several different educational regimes. From the governess's point of view, frequent changes of position made it difficult to establish exactly how and what children had learned before, and what level they had reached. Governesses were expected to provide a grounding in a range of subjects from basic reading and writing skills, through elementary grammar, history, and literature, to mathematics and natural history, including botany and entomology. In addition, the governess might have to supervise the children's amusements, including gardening, horse riding, and games. Though sporting interests were seldom encouraged in girls, light physical exercise was considered important. The governess was also expected to school older girls in the accomplishments: piano playing, embroidery, dancing, drawing and painting. Sometimes, visiting masters would provide specialist training in these areas. On the whole, however, full responsibility for the attainments of a young woman would fall on the governess, whose regime had necessarily, from the very start, included instruction in the most important areas of all: manners, morals, and the study of the Bible. Finally, events in the domestic classroom could not proceed smoothly if the governess was lax in inculcating discipline.

The demands of such a curriculum were extreme and the need for written guidance and particularly for textbooks for the schoolroom had never been

Fig. 6 Mrs Sarah Bennet: 'a Christian governess'.

greater. Despite the profusion of such aids, however, there were few firm guidelines as to exactly what and how children should learn. For governesses with little academic knowledge and no teacher training, the lack of regulation was open to abuse. Children often studied a hotchpotch of different subjects, largely dependent on the books that were available within the household. Provided their employers either didn't care or didn't notice, governesses could drop subjects in which they themselves did not feel confident, such as arithmetic or science. Lacking expertise in their task, they were often guilty of the most unimaginative methods of teaching, guaranteed to engender resentment among their pupils. On the other hand, for those governesses who rose to the challenge, there was, in this irregular system, the freedom to devise wide-ranging and elaborate lessons in which subjects such as history could be taught in conjunction with science, literature and even music; and in which the teacher could experiment with a number of different methods, both inside the classroom and without.

While getting to grips with the rigours of her curriculum, the governess also needed to adjust to her new living and working conditions. For Elizabeth Gould these appear to have been at once glamorous and rather lonely and inhospitable. In households where education was taken seriously and space was available, the governess would have a schoolroom and possibly a bedroom of her own. Manuals of domestic design of the period suggested ways in which the schoolroom might be made more conducive to study. Towards the end of the century, wealthy families even provided special transport for the governess and her pupils, such as a specially-designed carriage or 'governess cart'.

Though the governess's duties were primarily concerned with the instruction of the children and her province was the schoolroom, in less affluent households, the boundaries of her existence were not always so

Fig. 7 Working drawing of a governess car. Designed to be driven down narrow country lanes or on private estates, and to be drawn by a small pony or donkey, the governess car or cart was built with safety in mind. Sitting sideways on, the governess could keep an eye on her charges as she drove, though this made for an awkward driving position.

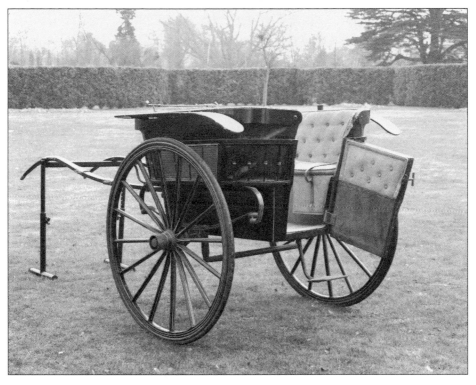

Fig. 8 This governess car is part of the Mossman Collection and can be seen at the Stockwood Craft Museum near Luton.

strictly drawn. Some governesses were compelled to take on tasks usually reserved for nursery maids or lady's maids, such as feeding and dressing the smallest children, or undertaking copious quantities of needlework. Occasionally, employers actually advertised for governesses on these terms, much to the chagrin of contemporary social commentators. In other households governesses would be presented on their arrival with unexpected duties, which they were hardly in a position to refuse. Such blurring of the distinctions between governesses and other servants made for the paradoxes of the governess's position which will be dealt with in Chapter 3.

Part 1:
Methods and Means

The late eighteenth and nineteenth centuries saw the publication of a huge number of textbooks for the use of governesses and later for schoolmistresses. It is impossible to know how widely these were used or how closely they were adhered to, but memoirs tell us that some, like Mrs Sherwood's The Fairchild Family (1818), became family favourites and remained so for generations. In many of these books, an emphasis is placed on rote learning and memory skills, techniques that are now regarded as mechanical, dreary and ineffective. However, the best textbook writers of the time succeeded in combining useful knowledge with an element of fun.

LEARNING THE BASICS

Fig. 9 'Spelling for Beginners'.

Sara Coleridge's Pretty Lessons in Verse for Good Children *(1834) from which the following poem is taken, was reissued many times during the Victorian era, sometimes with updated graphics and illustrations. Its popularity stemmed from its playful solutions to tricky problems of spelling, conduct and even Latin vocabulary. The benefits of learning verse as an aide-mémoire for spelling are self-evident, but the memorizing of information was also recommended for many other subjects, and here its value seems questionable. Successful textbooks addressed the needs of a double audience: first the governess herself, whose own*

EI AND IE.

 AID Ronald, beginning to fret,
"These words in *e i* and *i e!*
I ne'er could distinguish them yet,
They're terribly puzzling to me.

"They all are alike in their sound!
I ne'er shall the difference tell,
But one with the other confound—
'Tis troublesome learning to spell."

His father said thus in reply—
"The English words ending in *ceive*,
Where *e* must be put before *i*,
Your memory ne'er can aggrieve.

"Those words we from Latin receive;
From *capio* all of them come;
Their number is four, I believe,
And that is no very great sum.

"When this, my dear boy, you *perceive*
(A rule that will never *deceive*),
'Tis easy enough to *conceive*
What profit you thence will *receive*.

"And ne'er let it tease you,
My darling, I pray,
In *teize* should you meet with
Ei for *ea*.

"And ne'er let it *grieve* you
That in the word *sheik*,
The *e* is put foremost
Though hindmost in *shriek*.

"It comes first in *ceiling*,
And likewise in *seize*;
If this your mind seizes,
Your father 'twill please.

"It comes first in *teil*-tree,
In *feint* and in *teint*;
Now this on your mem'ry
Pray try to imprint."

education might have been sparse and whose training as an educator even more so, and secondly the pupils. The two geography lessons below demonstrate the question-and-answer routine, a popular and ancient method of teaching and the Church's favoured method of instructing the young in doctrinal matters. In the first example, a lesson about the Scandinavian countries is conducted by the governess who imparts to her pupil a series of carefully ordered fragments of factual information. The pupil is then questioned on the facts in the same order. In the second example, the governess supplements her teaching by referring to the terrestial and celestial globes, an elegant and versatile item of classroom equipment.

Norway, Sweden, and Lapland

[. . .]

1. Norway and Sweden, forming together one immense peninsula, upwards of fifteen hundred miles in length, are situated in the north-west part of Europe.

2. Through the greater portion of their extent these countries are separated by a lofty and rugged range of mountains, called the Dofrafield.

3. Several years since, Norway and Sweden were united into one kingdom, and became subject to a sovereign, who had formerly been one of Bonaparte's generals.

4. These countries are remarkably cold, barren, and mountainous; though the climate of Sweden is warmer than that of Norway.

5. In the most northerly parts, and in Lapland, which is subject to Sweden, the sun does not set for two months together during the summer, nor does it appear above the horizon for the same space of time during the winter. [. . .]

Questions on Chapter III

1. Of what form are Norway and Sweden? of what length? and how are they situated with regard to the rest of Europe?

2. How are Norway and Sweden naturally separated?

3. Are these countries under one or two separate governments?

4. What is the character of these countries in regard to their soil and climate?

5. For what are the days and nights during two months in summer, and two in winter, remarkable, in the more northerly parts of these countries, and in Lapland?

Questions on the Use of Globes

1. How many kinds of globes are there?

2. What is the difference between a globe and a map?

3. What is shewn on the face of a terrestial globe?

4. What is the real shape of the earth?

5. What is meant by the diameter of the earth? Supposing a globe to be made of the exact figure of the earth, what would be the difference between its longest and shortest diameter?

Figs 10 and 11 Originally designed and produced as navigational instruments, by the nineteenth century these elaborate globes would have been used as teaching aids in the schoolroom or to ornament a wealthy drawing room.

6. What is the axis of a globe?
7. What are the poles of the earth or of an artifical globe?
8. What is the name given to that part of the heavens opposite to the North Pole? What is the point opposite the South Pole called?
9. What is the Equator, and how is it situated?
10. How are circles divided by geometers? How many degrees are there in a circle? How many in a semi-circle? How many in a quadrant?

Charles Butler, *An Easy Guide to Geography and the Use of the Globes* (1846), pp. 16, 17, 191.

THE UBIQUITOUS MANGNALL

The best known – though not universally admired – of all the question-and-answer books published in the nineteenth century was probably Richmal Mangnall's Historical and Miscellaneous Questions *(1800). Although presented in a somewhat eccentric and rambling style, the questions and their answers were, of course, unapologetically ideological. Written in the wake of the French Revolution, they installed an element of self-righteous patriotism into the English curriculum that would survive for decades to come.*

Which four of our British queens have given the greatest proofs of courage and intrepidity? Boadicea, queen of the Iceni; Philippa, wife to Edward the 3rd; Margaret of Anjou, wife to Henry the 6th; and Elizabeth, who reigned in her own right. What English kings, since the conquest, have ascended the throne when minors? Henry the 3rd, Richard the 2nd, Henry the 6th, Edward the 5th, and Edward the 6th. What English kings have been most distinguished by their love of war and conquest? William the Conqueror, Richard the 1st, Edward the 1st, Edward the 3rd, and Henry the 5th. What is true glory? Active benevolence, fortitude to support the frowns of fortune, evenness of temper in prosperity, patience in affliction, contempt of unmerited injuries;

Fig. 12 Although in general competitiveness was frowned upon in girls, a well-memorized lesson might be modestly rewarded.

this is virtue, and the fame of virtuous actions can alone be called true glory. Name some of the antiquities in England. Picts wall, between Northumberland and Cumberland; Stonehenge, in Wiltshire, or circles of stones, where the druids worshipped; York minster; Westminster abbey and hall, with many Roman monuments, altars, and roads. Name the five greatest philosophers England has produced. Roger Bacon, Lord Bacon, the honourable Robert Boyle, sir Isaac Newton, and John Locke. Name the weak kings who have filled the English throne since the conquest. John, Henry the 3rd, Edward the 2nd, Richard the 2nd, Henry the 6th, and James the 2nd. What is meant by a patriot king? One who has his country's welfare particularly at heart, and studies the benefit of his subjects more than his own private interests.

Richmal Mangnall, *Historical and Miscellaneous Questions* (1800),

pp. 122–3.

So Much Useless Cram

By the middle of the century, with the growing interest both in childhood and teaching methods, textbooks such as Mangnall's slowly lost favour in the eyes of many commentators. Regimented question-and-answer routines, largely a legacy of late eighteenth-century pedagogy, were gradually replaced by procedures geared more closely to pleasure. Just two years before Charles Dickens's famous satire on fact-based learning in Hard Times *(1854), James Pycroft, in a letter on the education of girls written to* The Englishwoman's Domestic Magazine, *expressed his disapproval of old-fashioned teaching practices which did not consider the child as child. Here, Pycroft begins by modifying the idea familiar to writers and educators from John Locke and David Hartley onwards: that knowledge is achieved through associations of pleasure and pain.*

[. . . T]he great secret of education is to leave associations of pleasure, not of pain, connected with learning. 'Strong meats' to those who crave for 'milk' produce disgust and aversion, instead of growth and strength. 'The right thing at the wrong time' in education proves very poison; therefore avoid every book in the form of question and answer – Mangnall's 'Questions' or Pinnock's 'Catechisms' – as so much useless cram for the memory. They contain odds and ends of knowledge, which, since I could not at my present age digest anything in such a form, you can hardly expect to agree with the mental constitution of a child. Brewer's 'Guide to Science' is valuable to an adult, who could read it all in a day or two; but it has formed a year's torture to many a young girl, confirming a distaste for all science to the end of her days.

All such works owe their popularity to the fallacy that education means cramming – laying in a store of information, the same store to be drawn upon through after life. My own experience, no doubt, is that of all other persons. All my school store (save in language) has vanished years since, and the greater part I would not have again on any consideration.

James Pycroft, 'Your Daughter's Education' (1852), p. 81.

A MONSTER OF IGNORANCE

Such diatribes in the press were echoed in more subtle ways in classic fiction of the period, where the banalities and absurdities of the schoolroom became a staple of comedy. In Thackeray's The Newcomes *(1853–5), what appears to be an account of Ethel Newcome's capacities as a pupil affords a dig at the whole sytem of governessing and at those wealthy mothers who allowed their daughters' education to meander pointlessly along.*

[Lady Ann Newcome's] daughter had had so many governesses – all darlings during the first week, and monsters afterwards – that the poor child possessed none of the accomplishments of her age. She could not play on the piano; she could not speak French well; she could not tell you when gunpowder was invented; she had not the faintest idea of the date of the Norman Conquest, or whether the earth went round the sun, or vice-versâ. She did not know the number of counties in England, Scotland, and Wales, let alone Ireland; she did not know the difference between latitude and longitude. She had had so many governesses: their accounts differed; poor Ethel was bewildered by a multiplicity of teachers, and thought herself a monster of ignorance. They gave her a book at a Sunday School, and the little girls of eight years old answered questions of which she knew nothing. The place swam before her. She could not see the sun shining on their fair flaxen heads and pretty faces. The rosy little children holding up their eager hands, and crying the answer to this question and that, seemed mocking her. She seemed to read in the book, 'O Ethel, you dunce, dunce, dunce!'

[. . .]

When Ethel was thirteen years old, she had grown to be such a tall girl, that she overtopped her companions by a head or more, and morally perhaps, also, felt herself too tall for their society. 'Fancy myself,' she thought, 'dressing a doll like Lily Putland, or wearing a pinafore like Lucy Tucker!' She did not care for their sports, she could not walk with them: it seemed as if every one stared; nor dance with them at the academy; nor attend the Cours de Littérature Universelle et de Science Compréhensive of the professor then the mode – the smallest girls took her up in the class. She was bewildered by the multitude of things they bade her learn. At the youthful little assemblies of her sex, when, under the guidance of their respected governesses, the girls came to tea at six o'clock, dancing, charades, and so forth, Ethel herded not with the children of her own age, nor yet with the teachers who sit apart at these assemblies, imparting to each other their little wrongs; but Ethel romped with the little children – the rosy little trots – and took them on her knees, and told them a thousand stories. By these she was adored, and loved like a mother almost, for as such, the hearty kindly girl showed herself to them; but at home she was alone, *farouche*, and intractable, and did battle with the governesses and overcame them one after another.

William Makepeace Thackeray, *The Newcomes* (first published 1853–5, reprinted 1911), pp. 134–7.

RICHARD II WAS THOUGHTLESS AND PRODIGAL

By the 1860s, criticism of mechanical learning had extended even to children's fiction, where it had become synonymous with incompetent governessing. Julia Luard's popular Childhood and Schoolroom Hours of Royal Children *(1865), enacts the symbolic defeat of fact-based learning in the person of the ineffectual Miss Seymour, whose history lessons rely exclusively on Mangnall. Facing the recalcitrance of her charges – May, Gerald, Rose and Charlie – Miss Seymour becomes indisposed and retires to her bed. At this point, the children's Aunt May steps in to offer her own brand of history. The focus is still on kings and queens, but this time the lesson is a narrative and anecdotal account of royal childhoods – altogether more appealing and ultimately more memorable to the children.*

[. . .] Rose was weeping floods of tears over two pages of 'Little Arthur's History', which she had to read over again to herself more attentively; and May was fighting with 'Mangnall's Questions', and cavilling at every word, and of course not learning at all. Perhaps my readers are as anxious as Aunt May was to find out how this was managed, and therefore we will give an example: May's lesson consisted of a short summary of the reigns of Richard II, and Henry IV in 'Mangnall', and had, of course to be repeated word by word from the book. No very easy or interesting lesson, but which had been lately imposed on May, from Miss Seymour finding, to her dismay, that her pupil was grossly ignorant of the principal events belonging to each reign. May was naughty enough to be determined not to try to learn such 'a detestable lesson', as she called it, and never sat down to it without wishing in a loud whisper that 'that old *de*testable "Mangnall" was burnt'. To-day she went on worse than ever, and without lowering her voice proceeded in the following manner:

'"Richard II was thoughtless and prodigal", indeed, you think so, do you? (commented May in a scornful voice). Much you know about it. Thoughtless was he? I suppose he never thought about his little wife and how to educate her!

[. . .]

The next day a note came from Miss Seymour instead of herself, which told them that she was ill in bed from fatigue and headache. It was to very sober faces, to consciences full of self-reproach at their late conduct to Miss Seymour, that Aunt May announced herself as their governess, though smiles might have been discovered at her proposal to continue her stories of the childhood and schoolroom hours of royal children, 'but only on condition' said Aunt May, with marked emphasis, 'that you all do well the tasks I shall set you in history and take pains to write answers to the questions I shall give you on the selections I intend you to read from old histories.' [. . .] 'Hurrah,' they shouted, 'down with old Mangnall and up with Aunt May, Aunt May for ever!'

Julia Luard, *The Childhood and Schoolroom Hours of Royal Children*
(1865), pp. 133–8.

A Country Rectory in the 1860s

While contemporary fiction abounded in exaggerated depictions
of restrictive teaching practices – to satiric and comic effect –
tough routines were usually only a part of diverse and often
entertaining timetables. In the 1940s, Mary Paley Marshall,
widow of the academic Alfred Marshall and for many years a
lecturer in Economics in her own right, looked back on her
experiences of learning in the 1860s with fond amusement.

I can't remember much about our education till I was nine years old except that Mrs Markham's *History of England* was read aloud to us and Geography was learnt from two books *Near Home* and *Far Off*, and that we played scales on the piano. In 1859 a German governess came and more regular lessons began. History, it is true, was chiefly dates and we learnt them by a Memoria Technica, beginning 'Casibelud Boadorp', etc., and Geography was chiefly names of Towns and Rivers. But we were taught French and German pretty thoroughly and the family talked German at meals. Science we learnt from *The Child's Guide to Knowledge* and *Brewer's Guide*. All I now remember of these is the date at which black silk stockings came into England and 'What to do in a thunderstorm at night', the answer being: 'Draw your bed into the middle of the room, commend your soul to Almighty God and go to sleep.' We did a little Latin and even Hebrew with my father and some Euclid. As to story books, we read *The Wide Wide World*, *Holiday House*, *Henry and his Bearer*, and *Sandford and Merton*. On Sundays we learnt the church catechism, collects, hymns and Cowper's poems, there was a periodical called *Sunday at Home* and we read and re-read the *Pilgrim's Progress* and the *Fairchild Family*. This had a prayer and a hymn at the end of each chapter, and some children I knew took all the prayers and hymns at a gulp, so as to get them over and then freely enjoyed that entertaining book.

[. . .]

Regular education stopped when I was about thirteen, and our Fräulein married the chief farmer in the village. During the following year my sister and I went once a week to a select school for young ladies in our nearest town, kept by two maiden ladies, where we were taught 'Mangnall's Questions', the 'use of the globes' and deportment. Our education was then 'finished' and for the next two or three years we read and did much as we chose. [. . .]

Later on, when we were growing up, we spent much time at Scarborough. We had a father who took part in work and play and who was interested in electricity and photography, and a mother who was full of initiative and always bright and amusing. We owed much to our excellent German governess. She not only taught us French and German and some drawing and music, but brought variety into life. She played games and taught us to act little plays and charades, was always cheerful and we missed her greatly when she married. It was after she left and when the governess stage was past and we had no regular occupation that we began to feel bored, especially in winter.

Mary Paley Marshall, *What I Remember* (1947), pp. 6–8.

A Practical Approach

*Haphazard and diverting though the curriculum might appear
to have been in autobiographical accounts, advice to
governesses reiterated the importance of planning and method
in teaching. Since the publication of Maria and Richard Lovell
Edgeworth's* Practical Education *(1798), the need for children
to learn 'useful' subjects had been emphasized. As far as the
education of middle-class girls was concerned, it was regarded
as common sense that academic subjects should be pursued only
so far as they were relevant to future roles as wives, mothers
and domestic managers. In an anonymous booklet from the
1860s, 'an old governess' describes the teaching of arithmetic to
middle-class girls in a manner that makes such expectations
abundantly clear.*

[. . .] Now this is the next thing we have to say to you, as we could wish some one long ago had whispered it in our own ear, 'Teach the children to do, to use, and to understand those things which they will want to do, use, and understand, when they leave your care.' Teach them what you have felt the want of; what you have felt the benefit of. It is easy to say, 'Education should be made practical;' but we will come, a little more in detail, to what we mean.

We will suppose, then, that while your pupils' attention is fresh, near the beginning of the morning, you have a lesson in *Arithmetic*. – Ask Miss Louisa, who brought home that showy ciphering-book last half-year, with 'Simple Proportion,' 'Double Proportion,' 'Decimal Fractions', so beautifully printed in German text, or Old English, – ask her whether she can write out a grocer's or a draper's bill? Whether she knows the meaning of a post-office order, or a cheque? Whether she can calculate, – supposing her new dress takes fourteen yards of silk three-quarters wide, – how much she must buy of a silk only half-a-yard wide? Whether she can reckon, without the slate – nay, in the shop, and by the time it is measured off – five and a-half yards of ribbon, at ninepence half-penny, and how much change out of five

SIMPLE ADDITION.

New Governess. "WHY ARE YOU STARING SO INTENTLY, BLANCHE, DEAR?"
Blanche. "I WAS TRYING TO COUNT THE FRECKLES ON YOUR FACE, MISS SANDYPOLE, BUT I CAN'T!"

Fig. 13 *Punch*'s vision of schoolroom arithmetic (1871).

shillings? Many Miss Louisas cannot do these things, after years spent at lessons, for the simple reason that they are not regularly exercised in them. Why should not children, in their first, or soon after their first lessons, see and handle pence, shillings, and half-crowns (which will be as pleasant as it is useful to them), till they are familiar with their respective values? Do they not perform slate calculations, on purpose that they may be able to manage these very pence, shillings, and half-crowns? 'Oh, but that will all come to them, when they have to keep house.' By your leave, it does *not* always come to them. We have observed the young lady-wife in the market, paying what was asked, evidently confused, and unable to tell whether she was cheated or not.

Anon. *A Word to a Young Governess by an Old One*, (1860), pp. 11–13

PROBLEMS FOR YOUNG LADIES

*From the late eighteenth century, writers of textbooks for the
schoolroom were rising to the challenge of adapting academic
subjects to the supposed requirements of genteel femininity. The
mathematical exercises below, with their emphasis on shopping –
and the occasional bout of philanthropy – delineate the contours
of a world in which middle-class females were increasingly to be
cast as consumers rather than producers.*

1. Gave 10l. 15s. 4d. for 9 hats, what did one cost?
    Answer 1l. 3s. 11d.
2. How much does 1lb. of meat come to at 5s. 11d. per stone?
    Answer 8¾d.
3. Bought 10 yards of lace for 5l. 11s. 3¼d. how much is that per yard?
    Answer 11s. 1½d.
4. Divide twenty guineas among 13 persons.
    Answer 1l. 12s. 3½d.
5. Required the 16th part of 100 guineas.
    Answer 6l. 11s. 3d.
6. Paid 19s. 6d. for a cheese of 36lb. weight, required the price per pound.
    Answer 6½d.
7. If I pay my servant 18l. 18s. for a year, how much is that per
    week?
    Answer 7s. 3d.
8. 22 persons had a prize of one thousand pounds, tell me the share of
    each person?
    Answer 45l. 9s. 1d.
9. The clothing of a charity school, consisting of 35 children, came to
    57l. 3s. 7d. what is the expence of each?
    Answer 1l. 12s. 8d.
10. My cheesemonger has sent me a firkin of butter, price 1l. 19s. 11d.
    how much is that per pound?
    Answer 8½d.

[. . .]

A Bookseller's Bill

Stationers'-Court, March 1st 1814.

Mrs SOMERVILLE,

Bought of B. and R. CROSBY & Co.

	s	d
Rundall's Grammar of Sacred History	4	0
Elements of English Education, by Brown	5	6
Mrs Chapone's Letters on the Improvement of the Mind, 18mo. .	2	6
Dr Mavor's New Speaker, or English Class Book	4	6
Essays on Rhetoric, from Dr Blair	4	6
Tomkin's Select Poems	3	6
Evans's Sketch of All Religions, boards	3	6
Gay's Fables, with wood cuts, by Branston	3	6
Accomplished youth	2	6
Blair's Grammar of Chemistry	4	0
Walker's Elements of Geography, 8vo.	11	6
— Gazetteer, 8vo.	12	0
Death of Cain	2	6
Dr Watts's Improvement of the Mind	3	6
Charlotte Smith's Minor Morals, 2 vols.	5	4
Gregory's Advice to his Daughter	2	6
London Letter-Writer, bound in red	1	6
Economy of Human Life	3	6
Langhorne's Fables of Flora	5	4
Collins's Ready Reckoner in Miniature	1	3
Blair's Advice to Youth	2	0
Lowndes's History of England	5	0
Looking Glass for the Mind	3	6
Blossoms of Morality	3	6

£

John Grieg, *The Young Ladies' New Guide to Arithmetic* (1816), pp. 40–1, 15.

Classics for the Ladies

*The hypothetical bookseller's bill above is a revealing index of
what were considered desirable reading habits for middle-class
girls. Division of the curriculum along gender lines was common
practice in all but a few households, yet we must not be too ready
to universalize here. Though the classics were generally regarded
as the province of boys – awaiting them beyond the domestic
environment at public school – there were educational
commentators who also saw merits for females in the discipline of
learning Latin and Greek. Remember that Elizabeth Gould, whose
letter opened this chapter, noted that her nine-year-old pupil,
'knew a little Latin', and implied her own knowledge of the
language.*

It is very desirable, that little girls should learn Latin; and if they have
brothers, they will perhaps for some time, be associated with them in
their lessons; though it cannot be necessary, that the course pursued by
the two sexes should be the same, beyond a certain period. Indeed the
chief use of Latin to a lady, is to give her a knowledge of the principles
of grammar, the derivations of words, and the meaning of some of the
terms she may find in works of science.

S.F. Ridout, *Letters to a Young Governesss on the Principles of
Education* (1840), p. 77.

Before finally quitting the subject of classics we must say a few words
relative to teaching them to *girls*. We should advise, for *their* study, a
moderate amount of Latin, but *much* Greek. No ancient language is so
suited to female study as Greek, or contains so much that so quickly
rewards the learner. One can wish no happier or pleasanter intellectual
boon to a young lady than the power of reading the Gospels in the
original, or the delight of filling her mind with the ever-fresh glories of old
Homer. Girls, too, will take delight, when properly instructed, in the
straightforward simplicity and beauty of the clear Greek prose of

Xenophon, and the 'gossipry' of Herodotus; and they should be encouraged in their Greek bias, not merely by the knowledge that Greek is, on the whole, a far easier language than Latin, but that it is a *yet living dialect*, as soft, when rightly pronounced, as the most flowing Tuscan, and as forcible as the Greek of old. Indeed, a fair knowledge of *ancient* Greek makes the acquisition of the modern language a matter of a few weeks.

Anthony F. Thomson, *The English Schoolroom* (1865), pp. 273–4.

GRAMMAR FOR GOVERNESSES

If the governess's role was partly to consolidate gender ideals, she had also to reinforce demarcations of class. Often better spoken than those by whom she was employed, she was expected to iron out the inacccuracies, mispronunciations, and general slipshoddiness of a new generation of the bourgeoisie. Woe betide, on the other hand, any governess whose own speech betrayed lowly origins. In the exercises below, it is recommended that the governess correct her pupil's speech to a fine degree of detail.

I wish you and I *was* schoolfellows: if I *was* with you I am sure I *would* be so happy.

I wish you and I *were* schoolfellows: if I *were* with you I think I *should* be happy.

I *love* dancing. Don't you? For my part I *reckon upon* the dancing days very much.

Are you *fond* of dancing? It is an amusement I am very partial to; and I *anticipate* the pleasure I am to receive from the attendance of my master.

I have *learnt* drawing more than a year; but I cannot draw a landscape to please *myself* or my *master*.

I am sorry to say I have been *taught* drawing more than a year, without being able to *finish* a landscape in a manner that my master approves, or to please myself.

I have lost my doll's pretty bonnet that I took so much trouble to make, and I am quite *miserable* about it. I told the nurse she *must* find it for me.

I have met with a heavy loss. The doll's bonnet you saw me making the other day: mama said it was pretty; and I am *grieved* lest she should be angry with me for not taking better care of my things. I have *intreated* nurse to assist me in seeking for it.

If the candles are *lit* we had better go into the dancing-room.

If the candles are *lighted* we had better go into the dancing-room; but as you please.

I did not come to school yesterday, because mama *know'd* it would be *ill*-convenient to my governess to receive us.

I did not come to school yesterday, because mama *knew* that it would be *in*convenient to my governess to receive any of her pupils.

Was you in town last week? *me and my* sister *was*, and papa took us to see Blue Beard.

Were you in town last week? *my sister and I* were, when Papa had the goodness to take us with him to see Blue Beard.

That's a pretty *gound*: Miss Dawsons say *they're* going to buy *theirselves* one like it.

That is a pretty cotton your *gown* is made of: Miss Dawsons say *they* are going to buy some like it for *themselves*.

Helena Wells, *Letters on Subjects of Importance to the Happiness of Young Females* (1799), pp. 158–77.

A GLORIOUS MISCELLANY

In spite of the constraints of gender and class, there is evidence that, at her best, the nineteenth-century governess was remarkable for breadth of perspective, mental agility and imaginative use of limited resources. Here an anonymous advice writer, addressing her remarks to schoolmistresses and private governesses alike (p. 3), suggests something of the dexterity needed to weave together coherent lessons from the disparate materials available.

I would have a part of every afternoon spent in reading aloud, each reading by turns, while the rest work; taking history and miscellaneous reading on alternate afternoons. In reading history, at least with children under ten or twelve years of age, I would begin with the outline given in Mrs Cameron's most useful and interesting little 'Nursery Magazine' and then read the beautiful sketch called 'The Five Empires', before proceeding to particular histories, either of England or other countries, The little Magazine I have just mentioned supplies exceedingly well the *beginnings* of other branches of study, besides miscellaneous reading of a most suitable kind for young children.

On the alternate afternoons, I would generally choose subjects which would have some connection with the history read at the time, – referring perhaps to the country itself to which the history related, or to events and particular persons belonging to that country, or period of time. Thus I would sometimes have a book of suitable travels, or selected passages from such books; or a poem, or anecdotes of remarkable persons, or accounts of the work of missionaries. Maps should always be used at the same time, and in all we read, continual reference should be made to the Bible, and illustrations of its lessons, history, etc., pointed out as they occur.

Anon. *Hints to a Young Governess on Beginning a School*, (1857), pp. 28–9.

THE POSSIBILITIES OF THE MAY-FLY

*Even the catechistical method so discredited by Mangnall
could, in the hands of an astute and knowledgeable
governess, embrace wide-ranging possibilities. A popular
subject with middle-class girls was natural history,
particularly the developing sciences of botany and
entomology. Both were deemed more ladylike than the study
of the behaviour of animals (presumably because the latter
was more likely to engender awkward questions about
reproduction). In the dialogue below, the governess, using the
apparently unpromising subject of the may-fly as her starting
point, leads her pupil on a fascinating interdisciplinary
ramble.*

Governess: I shall tell you of the May-fly next.

Pupil: I suppose it is seen the most in May?

Governess: Yes; it takes its name from emerging from its torpidity in this month. The anglers make use of it as a bait. It is very short-lived: it becomes an insect about six o'clock in the morning, and dies before eleven at night.

Pupil: Poor thing – it does spend a short and merry life! You said that the fly is used as a bait: what fish will eat it?

Governess: It is the favourite of the trout. I was standing, one evening in May, by the river side, and, as I saw numbers of these insects sporting in perfect happiness, I silently offered up my praise to Him whose unlimited benevolence had created so many happy beings, when a hungry fish, delighted with the prospect of so large a repast, left his companions, and threw himself among the insects, just as a ravenous wolf would go into a sheep-fold.

Pupil: The hungry fish was a trout, I dare say.

Governess: Yes; no doubt. You, perhaps, pity the fly, on account of its short life; but as the poet says –

3. THE GIRL OF THE PERIOD BUTTERFLY (*Fuella rapidula*).

Fig. 14 The contemporary obsession with entomology in the schoolroom prompted this flight of fancy in *Punch* (1870).

'Nor too brief the date of thy cheerful race –
'Tis its use that measures time –
And the Mighty Spirit, that fills all space
With His life and His will sublime,
May see that the May-fly and the man
Each flutter out the same small span;
And the fly that is born with the sinking sun,
To die ere the midnight hour,
May have deeper joy ere his course be run
Than man in his pride and pow'r;
And the insects' minutes be spared the fears
And the anxious doubts of our three-score years.'

Pupil: If they are so short-lived, I should think they are not so numerous.
Governess: They are numerous beyond description. The air near the rivers on the continent is so full of them, that Reamur, in his Travels, tells us that, on the banks of the Seine, the ground is covered with these flies three and four inches deep.

Pupil: Is not the Seine in France?

Governess: Yes; and from these flies being so numerous, the farmers there gather them in cart-loads, for manure.

Pupil: As they do sprats sometimes in England, I suppose?

Governess: I have heard they do the same in Carniola.

Pupil: I do not remember reading of Carniola in my geography.

Governess: I think you must. Is it not a duchy in Germany, near Hungary, and subject to Austria?

Pupil: You have not told me the colour of these insects.

Governess: They are of a greenish brown, with transparent wings elegantly mottled.

Mary Bristow Wood, *The Entomological Researcher* (1845), pp. 12–15.

ACCOMPLISHMENTS

According to satirical accounts in novels and in the press, the academic competence of the governess was often of less importance to middle-class families than her ability to instruct in the so-called 'accomplishments'; music, drawing, dancing, embroidery and polite conversation. Talents in these areas were popularly portrayed as the currency needed by middle-class girls in the marriage market. As such, where mention was made of 'accomplishments' in advice literature, the term invariably carried overtones of vanity and frivolity. An education in accomplishments was usually contrasted unfavourably with instruction in morals and manners. Proper cultivation of the intellect was popularly seen to be at odds with the self-aggrandisement and superficiality associated with the 'accomplished' woman.

Yet a close examination of prescriptive works of the period suggests that accomplishments were derided only where they came to supersede all other attainments. As the following three passages suggest, training in these skills might elevate the mind

*to moral and spiritual purity in ways that academic subjects
could not. It is possible that advice writers also recognized the
fact that for those governesses who were themselves ladies
'fallen on hard times', instructing in the accomplishments was
far less daunting, and perhaps far less demeaning, than some of
the gruelling academic exercises they were expected to
undertake.*

Teaching Music: Science and Sensibility

MY DEAR S . . . .

Music affords a very delightful recreation, and where there is any
taste for it, we ought to cultivate and improve the talent; but I cannot
help regretting, that young people are sometimes compelled to pass
many hours in a pursuit, for which they have little or no natural
predilection, and in which, consequently, they never attain to much
proficiency. You will, probably, not be called on to decide, whether the
children under your care, shall learn Music; and you may, at all events,
desire to have some hints on the best mode of teaching it.

A little book, entitled 'Letters to a Young Pianoforte Player,' contains
very valuable instructions on fingering, the position of the hands, the
touch, and the expression, which characterize the truly graceful player;
and it is a pity, that these points are not always attended to, from the
very commencement; for bad habits are soon contracted, and a
common, or vulgar mode of playing insensibly prevails, to the
perversion of the taste.

Music takes a place in the education of a little girl, that is very
advantageous. As much time is necessary, to the attainment of dexterity
in the mechanical part, you can often so employ an hour that has no
other engagement.

I do not think it desirable for little children to be made to practise,
(as it is called) long together; there cannot be variety enough in their
exercises to keep the attention alive; and the consequence is weariness,
which gives rise to disgust. I would also recommend you to connect,
with the practice, a gradual introduction to the science of Music. Time

Fig. 15 Music lessons at the piano.

and tune may be considered the fundamental principles, upon which every variety of musical sound is based. Now, to give a very young child a perception of these, you should use your own voice, as the very best of instruments, for illustrating the proportionate length of notes, and difference of measures, as well as the variations of tone. The reading of music must be rendered extremely simple, at first; and should not be attempted until some facility has been gained in the use of the fingers.

I would recommend you Dr Callcott's 'Musical Grammar', or Burrowes's 'Thorough Bass Primer,' as elementary works on musical science. But my love for this delightful pursuit, induces me to make some observations, that you are not likely to find in any printed treatise; and which may be interesting to you, as a musician, though not applicable to the children at the period of education we are at present considering. Our gracious God has connected a sensibility to sweet sounds, with some of the most delightful feelings of the breast. Should not the talent then be cultivated to his glory, and exercised in his praise? Ought we to consider Music merely as an attractive accomplishment, which we may exhibit in certain circles for the gratification of our vanity? It should rather, I think, be our aim, to make it a refreshing, elevating recreation; the stimulant to amiable, benevolent, or devotional feeling, and the true effective expression of the language of the heart.

Few children are capable of so refined an enjoyment as this; but their taste will be formed on yours; and you should always endeavour to associate with Music, such recollections as shall be salutary and agreeable. I would not, on any account, confine young people to the practice of sacred music. National and pastoral airs abound, that are both pleasing and unexceptionable; and of late, a considerable number of compositions have appeared, that combine elegance with harmony, and words consistent with moral truth.

S.F. Ridout, *Letters to a Young Governesss on the Principles of Education* (1840), pp. 82–5.

Faithful Portraiture

There is an essential difference between the arts of music and drawing as regards the aptitude of the pupil. It has been stated that a musical ear is found to exist in two out of three children, though only half that number possess it in sufficient perfection to qualify them for performers; but up to a certain point, the faculty of drawing is enjoyed by every body who does not labour under some defect of vision, or infirmity of hand. This will appear a startling proposition to many, but we think that a little reflection will show that it is correct.

[. . .]

In the study of trees the pupil's first endeavour should be limited to faithful portraiture: foliage in its rich and massy forms can never be given till the art is acquired of drawing single trees with accuracy: five out of six are content if they can convey a general idea by a confused, blotchy kind of intermixture of light and shadow, with little regard to distinctness of form: it certainly may not be actually necessary to write underneath 'this is a tree,' but beyond an intelligible intimation that the marks do not mean a donkey or a pig, or a church steeple, such sketches entirely fail of their object. The pupil should commence with copying exactly the trunk and branches of a leafless tree, and proceed by well defining each separate mass of which its full foliage is composed. The shading ought not to be attempted till these outlines are complete.

George Stephen, *Guide to Service: The Governess* (1844),
pp. 239, 250–1.

The Work of Finishing

No part of the work of a governess is more important than that of forming the minds of elder pupils. Reading good authors with them is one great means to this end – such works, for example, as those on 'Mental and Moral Philosophy,' 'Bacon's Essays,' Coleridge's 'Aid to Reflection,' or Butler's 'Analogy.' Desultory and light reading should always be discouraged – good poetry does not fall under this censure – but that light literature of the day which destroys the taste for solid study. Much will depend on the books which girls see in the hands of their governess; if she set them the example of reading sentimental poetry or novels, they will not be backward in imitating her example. Attempts at composition should be encouraged, because mental activity is excited, and nothing more effectually shows a person her own want of power than these trials. Essays are often given by those who have no real acquaintance with the human mind as the first work to be done, whereas these being generally written on abstract subjects, it is the most absurd method to adopt. All affectation in writing should be discouraged, and mere imitation of others. A single description of a walk or a drive, or of some object in nature, is better than the most elaborate piece of flowery young-lady writing that was ever exhibited.

[Mary Maurice], *Governess Life: Its Trials, Duties and Encouragements*
(1849), pp. 96–7.

THE REDOUBTABLE BECKY SHARP

Needless to say, such exalted standards and achievements were easier to attain in theory than in practice, both for pupils and their hard-pressed teachers. The gap between what was possible and what was likely inspired novelists such as William Makepeace Thackeray, whose anti-heroine Rebecca Sharp is every employer's nightmare. Thackeray's own daughters, Anny and Minny, had seen off governesses aplenty, as their father searched in vain for 'a paragon' (Gérin, 1981). Here is Becky Sharp at work.

With the young people, whose applause she thoroughly gained, her method was pretty simple. She did not pester their young brains with too much learning, but, on the contrary, let them have their own way in regard to educating themselves; for what instruction is more effectual than self-instruction? The eldest was rather fond of books, and as there was in the old library at Queen's Crawley a considerable provision of works of

Fig. 16 Miss Sharp in her schoolroom.

light literature of the last century, both in the French and English languages (they had been purchased by the Secretary of the Tape and Sealing Wax office at the period of his disgrace), and as nobody ever troubled the bookshelves but herself, Rebecca was enabled agreeably, and, as it were, in playing, to impart a great deal of instruction to Miss Rose Crawley.

She and Miss Rose thus read together many delightful French and English works, among which may be mentioned those of the learned Dr Smollett, of the ingenious Mr Henry Fielding, of the graceful and fantastic Monsieur Crébillon the younger, whom our immortal poet Gray so much admired, and of the universal Monsieur de Voltaire. Once, when Mr Crawley asked what the young people were reading, the governess replied 'Smollett'. 'Oh, Smollett,' said Mr Crawley, quite satisfied. 'His history is more dull, but by no means so dangerous as that of Mr Hume. It is history you are reading?' 'Yes,' said Miss Rose; without however, adding that it was the history of Mr Humphrey Clinker. On another occasion he was rather scandalised at finding his sister with a book of French plays; but as the governess remarked that it was for the purpose of acquiring the French idiom in conversation, he was fain to be content. Mr Crawley, as a diplomatist, was exceedingly proud of his own skill in speaking the French language, (for he was of the world still), and not a little pleased with the compliments which the governess continually paid him upon his proficiency.

Miss Violet's taste were, on the contrary, more rude and boisterous than those of her sister. She knew the sequestered spots where the hens layed their eggs. She could climb a tree to rob the nests of the feathered songsters of their speckled spoils. And her pleasure was to ride the young colts and to scour the plains like Camilla. She was the favourite of her father and of the stable-men. She was the darling, and withal the terror of the cook; for she discovered the haunts of the jam-pots, and would attack them when they were within her reach. She and her sister were engaged in constant battles. Any of which peccadilloes, if Miss Sharp discovered, she did not tell them to Lady Crawley, who would have told them to the father, or, worse, to Mr Crawley; but promised not to tell if Miss Violet would be a good girl and love her governess.

With Mr Crawley Miss Sharp was respectful and obedient. She used to consult him on passages of French which she could not understand, though her mother was a Frenchwoman, and which he would construe to her satisfaction: and, besides giving her his aid in profane literature, he was kind enough to select for her books of a more serious tendency, and address to her much of his conversation. She admired, beyond measure, his speech at the Quashimaboo-Aid Society; took an interest in his pamphlet on malt; was often affected, even to tears, by his discourses of an evening, and would say – 'Oh, thank-you, sir,' with a sigh, and a look up to heaven, that made him occasionally condescend to shake hands with her. 'Blood is everything, after all,' would that aristocratic religionist say. 'How Miss Sharp is awakened by my words, when not one of the people here is touched. I am too fine for them – too delicate. I must familiarise my style – but she understands it. Her mother was a Montmorency.'

William Makepeace Thackeray, *Vanity Fair* (first published 1847–8, 1849), pp. 80–1.

THE FROLIC OF JUVENILE SPIRITS

The governess was often expected to superintend activities outside the classroom. While girls' pursuits were expected to be more sedentary than their brothers', a little gentle exercise and fresh air was highly recommended, at least before the onset of puberty. Anne Brontë's Agnes Grey had the unenviable task of trying to curb the boyish spirits of Miss Matilda Murray while encouraging her more fragile sister, Rosalie, to take the air. Advice works were correspondingly aware of the delicate balance to be struck by governesses in this sensitive matter.

All 'mammas' have an instinctive horror of their girls becoming *romps*: so far as this implies a boisterous, familiar, and therefore vulgar maturity, the antipathy is well-founded; but it is an error to assume that a hoydenish character is the necessary consequence of childish freedom; premature restraint and caution needlessly early, usually generate the very fault attributed to the opposite extreme: there are cases undoubtedly, in which a girl of even nine or ten, cannot prudently be permitted to indulge in the frolic to which juvenile spirits are naturally given; but these cases are exceptions to the general rule, and a mother should not be too anxious to find her daughter 'an exception:' it is a common failing; all parental affection is in favour of a child being 'an exception'; 'my Amelia is not a common girl' is the phrase in every maternal mouth, and a very absurd phrase it commonly is. Girls to the age of thirteen may be permitted to indulge at pleasure in play and exercise proportionate to their strength, with as little restraint as their brothers. We would not send them into the cricket-ground, nor initiate them in a game at football, because there is a sociality of intercourse in such plays that is not feminine in its nature; but we would not preclude them from exercise as strong, and as unrestrained, merely because it implied an effort of physical power; nor would we shut them out from the principal games of the boys of their own age, who are usually brothers or near relatives, on any principle of precocious prudery, so long as such games are not dangerous or indecorous; if they are, then they as unfit for the brother as for the sister. We love to see girls of eleven or twelve trundling a hoop, or running a garden-race, in rivalry with Tom just returned from Eton. We could even mention some of matronly dignity, and who wear their honours with becoming grace, who in earlier life could compete with ourselves in climbing a tree, or leaping over a brook.

George Stephen, *A Guide to Service: The Governess* (1844),
pp. 252–3.

OH! SO STRICT!

*In addition to her academic duties, the governess was responsible
for the discipline of the children. Some governesses inevitably
carried strictness too far. Mary Gladstone's diaries attribute her
lifelong lack of confidence in part to her governess of the 1850s
and 1860s, who constantly criticized and never praised or*

Fig. 17 'Subtle Discrimination.'

encouraged her. (Cited in Horn, 1997, p. 43.) On the other hand, teachers themselves could be sorely tried. Given the range of provocations available to pupils – witness the behaviour of Blanche Ingram and her brother towards their governesses in Jane Eyre, *recounted in Chapter 3 below – the governess's repertoire of punishments was relatively narrow, conditioned as it was by both ladylike decorum and her ambiguous place in the household. The need to instil respect and good behaviour seems to have been one of the chief areas of conflict between the teacher and her employer. In default of other effective means of controlling her charges, the governess often resorted to imaginative uses of the household spaces available to her (fig. 17). Mary Elizabeth Lucy remembered chastisements in the schoolroom with horror.*

My governess's name was Blackburn, she was very handsome and very good, but so strict. Oh! so strict! She used at first to frighten my wits away. I began lessons at six o'clock in summer and seven in winter, and had to forfeit a penny for every five minutes I was behind time. Breakfast was at eight, a bowl of bread and milk and nothing else until I entered my teens. And from that day I have never so much as tasted bread and milk. There was a closet in the schoolroom where we kept our exercise books and where Miss Blackburn had a loaf of bread, a slice of which she used to eat for her luncheon. Whenever I was turned with [stuck in] my lesson or showed the least sign of rebellion and temper or impatience, she would shut me up in this closet, which I dreaded above everything as I was so afraid of the mice that used to come after her bread, and were legion. And there I had to remain till I could say with a cheerful voice that I was quite good. She was really *over*-strict for if I only missed a word in repeating perhaps a page of history or a long piece of poetry she would often double the punishment. Ellin was in the schoolroom with me and, poor little soul, was forever in the closet.

Mary Elizabeth Lucy, *Mistress of Charlecote: The Memoirs of Mary Elizabeth Lucy* (written 1880s, 1987), pp. 16–17.

Part 2:
Conditions and Contexts

The daily life of the governess was determined as much by the context as
by the content of her teaching. In her private writings and those of social
commentators, the merits of a governess's post were evaluated with
regard to two matters in particular, namely what was demanded of her
beyond the confines of the schoolroom, and the quality of her
surroundings.

In respect of the first, the nature of the governess's tasks within the
household was important in distinguishing her from the servants. In the
course of the nineteenth century, middle-class families increasingly
demonstrated their wealth by extending their retinue of paid domestic
employees. As a consequence, attempts were made in a number of
household manuals to demarcate the roles of different kinds of servant
more clearly, and to clarify the respective obligations of householders
and their staff. In *The Rights, Duties and Relations of Domestic
Servants and their Masters and Mistresses*, T. Henry Baylis discussed the
position of 'menials' including, 'housekeepers, cooks, kitchenmaids,
housemaids, nurses, butlers, valets, coachmen, footmen, grooms,
gardeners [and] huntsmen'. Offering alternative derivations of the term
'menial', the first from the Latin 'intra moenia' meaning 'within the
walls', the second from the Saxon, 'meni' or 'moenig' or the Norman
'meing' meaning 'train, retinue, or, family', Baylis singled out the
governess as an exception, stating that 'though she live in the house
[she] does not come under that denomination' (1873, 4th ed. pp. 1–2).

*This distinction between governess and servants may have been clearer in
theory than in practice. In smaller households the tasks of the governess,
many of them suspiciously similar to the 'menial' duties of other servants,
often spilled outside the classroom and extended beyond teaching hours.
In July 1812, Ellen Weeton recorded the hard and unremitting labour
required over and above her strictly educational role in her daily
superintendence of the Armitage children of Liversedge, Yorkshire.*

A Hectic Day

My time is totally taken up with the children; from 7 o'clock in the morning, till half past 7, or 8 at night. I cannot lie any longer than 6 o'clock in a morning; and, if I have anything to do for myself, in sewing, writing, &c., I must rise sooner. At 7, I go into the nursery, to hear the children their prayers, and remain with them until after they have breakfasted, when I go out with them whilst they play; and am often so cold, that I join in their sports, to warm myself. About half past 8, I breakfast with Mr & Mrs Armitage, and then return again to the children till 9, when we go into the school-room till 12. We then bustle on our bonnets, &c., for play, or a short walk. At One, we bustle them off again, to dress for dinner, to which we sit down at a quarter past; the children always dine with their parents. By the time dinner is well over, it is 2 o'clock, when we go into school, and remain till 5. Whilst I am at tea in the parlour, the children eat their suppers in the nursery. I then go to them, and remain with them till 7, either walking out of doors, or playing within, as the weather may permit. I then hear their prayers, and see them washed; at half past 7, they are generally in bed.

Ellen Weeton, *Miss Weeton's Journal of a Governess*, (written 1811–25, reprinted 1969) Vol. 2, p. 58.

OCEANS OF NEEDLEWORK

The distinction most frequently ignored by employers was that between the work of the governess and that of the nanny or nurse. The existence of terms such as 'nursery governess' suggests that the mingling of roles was quite common; nevertheless, the requirement for governesses to supervise small children remained a bugbear of the profession. One correspondent to The Times *in January 1857 complained that she had been interviewed for a job as a governess only to find that she was expected to 'take entire charge of all the children, seven in number, two being quite babies; to perform for them all the menial offices of a nurse, make and mend their clothes; to teach at least three accomplishments, and "fill up the leisure hours of an evening by playing to company"'.*
('A Poor Governess', The Times, *20 January 1857, p. 12)*

After childcare, the most regularly bemoaned responsibility of the governess outside the schoolroom was that of household mending: an activity which carried its own connotations of drudgery. Because the governess was partly employed to teach sewing, knitting and even embroidery to young girls, employing the needle to more practical purposes was considered by many mothers to be a natural extension of her duties. Those contemporary commentators who sympathized with the 'plight' of the governess, however, found the requirement for her to undertake domestic sewing (rather than the more genteel fancywork which would have

Fig. 18 Nursemaid or governess?

attested to her accomplishments) rather distasteful. As Anthony Thomson put it in The English Schoolroom *(1865), 'it is a hard fate to be an angel of virtue, propriety and piety, combining therewith a knowledge of almost everything, yet having no repugnance to mending stockings . . .' (p. 71) The familiar overlap between governessing and needlework enhanced the pathos of the governess's role in the popular imagination, for the sempstress was, in her own right, an object of national pity. In a letter to a friend, Charlotte Brontë expresses her frustration at being required to undertake such tasks. It is likely, however, that many governesses considered a moderate amount of needlework an acceptable part of their role.*

I have striven hard to be pleased with my new situation. The country, the house, and the grounds are, as I have said, divine; but, alack-a-day! there is such a thing as seeing all beautiful around you – pleasant woods, white paths, green lawns, and blue sunshiny sky – and not having a free moment or a free thought left to enjoy them. The children are constantly with me. As for correcting them, I quickly found that was out of the question; they are to do as they like. A complaint to the mother only brings black looks on myself, and unjust, partial excuses to screen the children. I have tried that plan once, and succeeded so notably, I shall try no more. I said in my last letter that Mrs — did not know me. I now begin to find she does not intend to know me; that she cares nothing about me, except to contrive how the greatest possible quantity of labour may be got out of me; and to that end she overwhelms me with oceans of needlework; yards of cambric to hem, muslin nightcaps to make, and, above all things, dolls to dress. I do not think she likes me at all, because I can't help being shy in such an entirely novel scene, surrounded as I have hitherto been by strange and constantly changing faces.

Elizabeth C. Gaskell, *The Life of Charlotte Brontë* (1857), Vol. 1,
pp. 187–94.

VINCENT NOVELLO'S DAUGHTER

If the drudgery required of the governess detracted from her status as lady, so too did the demands made on her 'free' time. From autobiographical accounts of the governess life, it would appear that distinctions between work and leisure were often negligible. M. Jeanne Peterson records that on her 'days off', the resident teacher was drafted into a host of activities, including chaperoning, shopping, and reading aloud to her students (1972, p. 8). Moreover, as a lady of accomplishments, the governess might suffer the attentions of the family in the evening. For Mary Cowden-Clarke, whom we met in Chapter 1, invitations to appear before company and to perform with her pupils could be excruciating.

Fig. 19 In Richard Dadd's 'The Music Lesson, or The Governess' (1855), the governess's sombre grey attire contrasts starkly with her pupil's low-necked gown, which is vivid yellow and decked with crimson bows.

One of my chief anxieties while I was a governess was lest my pianoforte teaching and playing should not fulfil the expectation of my employers; for whenever I was requested to come up to the drawing-room and play a duet with either of my pupils, the second one always executed her part with unusual carelessness, infinitely less well than she played at other times. I remember especially one evening when I suffered an agony of nervousness while playing with Miss Celia an arrangement for four hands of the fine overture to Weber's 'Freischütz' (which overture, by-the-bye, had the unprecedented compliment of being invariably encored at the theatre this first season of the opera's being brought out in London), for we both played so miserably that I pictured to myself the company in the drawing-room saying, 'Can this be Vincent Novello's daughter?'

Mary Cowden-Clarke, *My Long Life* (1896), p. 33.

A COMPETENT MINISTER

Though dependent, in part, on the composition of the household staff, the extent of the governess's responsibilities also varied according to the mother's interpretation of her own role. Writers of manuals for mothers, confounded by the respectability and middle-class status of the governess, struggled to be even-handed about the balance of power to be held in the schoolroom. While the passage below evinces concern for the conditions in which the governess worked and takes care to differentiate her from the schoolroom maid, the writer also encourages an element of calculation on the part of the employer, suggesting that mothers delegate the more unpleasant of their maternal duties to the governess. Although the writer strives to be fair to the governess and advocates companionship between employee and employer, the governess remains a 'viceroy' and 'competent minister', whose duties will always remain ultimately under the jurisdication of the lady of the house.

Tea in the schoolroom is often, too, a very good institution, for thus the governess sees a little more of life, and acts as hostess; and each child should have its own cup and saucer and plate. This is a great safeguard against breakages, for if one is smashed it must be spoken of at once, and extra cups can be kept for the visitors; but all should be different, so that any breakage may be seen at once, as generally the schoolroom maid is but young, and apt to conceal any small depredations among the crockery. Now the two great difficulties in a schoolroom are the governess and the schoolroom-maid, and infinite care must be taken in the selection of both. Of course the governess is the first care, and though she should be mistress in the schoolroom, she yet must only be a viceroy, and must act for the mother entirely, and not at all on her own responsibility unless she is expressly desired to do so. No governess should be engaged who cannot be in some measure a companion to the mother, to whom and with whom she should be in perfect accord; for there are endless ways in which the governess can save a mother of a household, does she make herself really pleasant, if only in conveying the children to the dentist – a necessary business, but one that need not harrow the mother's feelings if the governess is as good and useful as she ought to be; for the governess does not feel, as a mother does, that all her teeth are being taken out bodily the moment Tommy opens his mouth for inspection, and endures none of the vicarious pangs that make any fanciful mother's life a burden to her, even though nothing happens. The governess must be healthy, strong-minded, good-tempered, and, above all, must have some nice hobbies, and be fond of teaching them; then the schoolroom will indeed be the heart of the house, and will send out a series of healthy, happy children into the great world. Make the governess one with the household; let your interests be hers, the children for the time being a mutual possession. Take any amount of trouble to procure a really nice girl of a good family, and then you may breathe freely; while if the schoolroom-maid comes young too, and is carefully trained, you will then have a perfectly managed schoolroom, and feel you can rest awhile should you desire it, secure that your place is well filled by a competent minister, who will rule in your place until you return both well and wisely.

J.E. Panton, *From Kitchen to Garret: Hints for Young Householders* (1888), pp. 199–200.

A Trip to the Museum

As we have seen, the governess could be whisked outside the precincts of the schoolroom to perform for guests, or to undertake household errands at the whim of her employer; but with a little initiative, she could also provide her own sound educational reasons for extending the limits of her environs. Walks in the garden or park punctuated with instructive conversation were a regular feature of textbooks for children from the late eighteenth century onwards. The 'object lessons' so important to nineteenth-century teaching were more fruitfully carried out in the natural environment than in the classroom. For those governesses working in or near towns, a trip to a museum or art gallery offered similar educational advantages.
In Charlotte Yonge's Hopes and Fears, *the governess, Miss Fennimore, initially opposes an unsupervised trip to London for her eldest charge.*

'I wonder what mamma said!' exclaimed Phoebe, in her strong craving for sympathy in her suspense.

'I am sorry the subject has been brought forward, if it is to unsettle you, Phoebe,' said Miss Fennimore, not unkindly; 'I regret your being twice disappointed; but if your mother should refer it to me, as I make no doubt she will, I should say that it would be a great pity to break up our course of studies.'

'It would only be for a little while, sighed Phoebe; 'and Miss Charlecote is to show me all the museums. I should see more with her than ever I shall when I am come out; and I should be with Robert.'

'I intended asking permission to take you through a systematic course of lectures and specimens when the family are next in town,' said Miss

Fennimore. 'Ordinary, desultory sight-seeing leaves few impressions; and though Miss Charlecote is a superior person, her mind is not of a sufficiently scientific turn to make her fully able to direct you. I shall trust to your good sense, Phoebe, for again submitting to defer the pleasure till it can be enhanced.

[...]

Phoebe took a sober walk with Miss Fennimore, receiving advice on methodically journalizing what she might see, and on the scheme of employments that might prevent her visit from being a waste of time.

Charlotte M. Yonge, *Hopes and Fears* (1899), pp. 113–16.

Fig. 20 An enterprising governess could bring the rather dry history lessons of the schoolroom to life by an excursion to a museum.

A SAMPLE OF THE MIND

The social and sexual contradictions inherent in the governess's role, which shall be examined in detail in Chapters 3 and 6, ensured that every aspect of her life from the moment she awoke until she retired to bed were the object of social concern and minute scrutiny. Even so apparently innocuous a question as what to wear occasioned elaborate advice.

The dress of a governess should depend on the habits of the family in which she resides. In some situations, more attention to appearance is required than in others; but, when this is left to her own choice, the simplest attire, well made, but never showy, is always in the best taste. Many entertain the notion that they insure respect by dressing much beyond their position in life; but this is a great mistake. Often, when so much is expended on the exterior, the general state of the wardrobe little corresponds with it.

Consistency is an estimable quality, and always pervades the character, influencing the most minute detail of habits, manners, and appearance. Want of taste or of perception sometimes misleads ladies in these things, and is seen in a bad combination of colours, or in the selection of those peculiarly unbecoming to them; or vulgarity of mind may lead them to suppose that their interests will be advanced by a gaudy exterior; but a sensible mother would recoil from what she would fairly judge to be a sample of the mind of the governess.

[Mary Maurice], *Governess Life: Its Trials, Duties and Encouragements* (1849), pp. 71–2.

Fig. 21 'The Governess who Ma said wouldn't do'. (*Punch*, 1893)

A ROOM FOR THE GOVERNESS

If the governess was constrained even in the choice of her own dress, there was one area in which she might recoup some authority, and this was in the organization of her schoolroom. As Emily Peart advised in her Book for Governesses *(1869), 'we are going to speak about duty . . . , and you are in your schoolroom: it is* yours *for the time – realize that; it is where God has placed you; it is your workroom, where you are to learn the joy of labour; your arena, where all that is most manly and most womanly in you is to be called into play; your battle-field, where toil is to be borne, effort to be made, difficulties overcome, and victory accomplished' (p. 26). In larger homes, the governess might hold sway over a suite of rooms grouped in one wing of the house. In Robert Kerr's 1865 book on the design of the English mansion, the location of the governess's bedroom expresses something of her position in the household as a whole. She resides among the younger members of the family, presumably so that she might more easily and comfortably carry out her domestic and quasi-maternal duties. At the same time, contemporary architectural principles may have exacerbated the governess's difficulties: her sense of isolation from family life, for example, and the problem of extricating herself from the persistent demands of the children.*

School-room and Suite

This is the name given to the apartment which is appropriated to two or three children withdrawn from the Nursery and placed under the care of a governess. In ordinary cases it will be not merely the Study, but also the Day-room of the pupils, and in some degree the Sitting-room of the governess.

A complete *School-room Suite* consists of the School-room itself, a Governess's-room adjoining, a private entrance-lobby if possible, a Washing-closet, &c., and perhaps a book-closet as better than a press in the School-room.

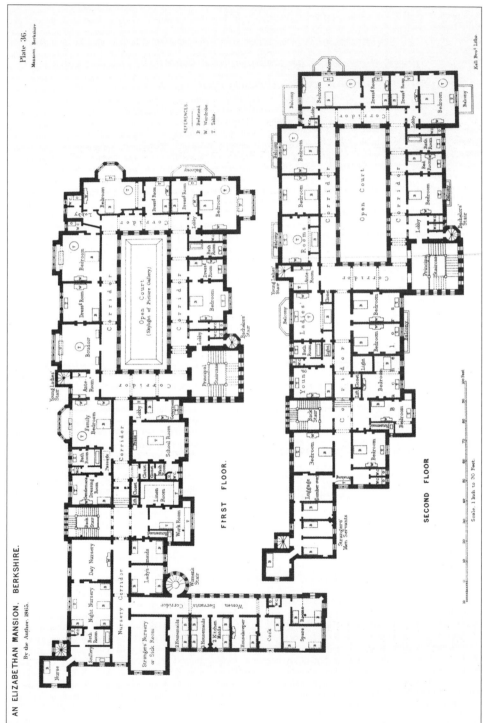

AN ELIZABETHAN MANSION. BERKSHIRE.

By the Author. 1865.

FIRST FLOOR.

SECOND FLOOR

Plate 36.

Mansom Berkshire

REFERENCES.

B Bedstead
W Wardrobe
T Table

Scale. 1 Inch to 30 Feet.

Fig. 22.

90

Figs. 22 and 23 Bear Wood House in Berkshire. This magnificent residence, designed by
Robert Kerr according to the ideals outlined in his book *The Gentleman's House* (1865),
included a special suite for the children and their teacher. However, few house plans,
except the most grandiose, included a room dedicated to the governess's personal use.

The *position* ought properly to be within easy reach of the lady of the
house; in other respects a place amongst the Bedrooms will almost
always be appropriate. The Nurseries need not be further off than may
be otherwise necessary. The same Staircase may serve for both
departments. The School-room, however, ought not to be above the First
Floor if possible; if a position on the Ground Floor can be had (as lately
suggested for the Day Nursery), so much the better, although that is
seldom to be hoped for. The Governess's-room, if not adjoining, ought
to be as near as possible: and the Bedrooms of the young ladies also
ought to be not too far removed from the Governess's-room.

[. . .]

A complete Suite of the kind above indicated is obviously convertible
into a *Bedchamber-Suite* when not in use, the Bed-room, Dressing-room,
private lobby, &c., being exactly as they ought to be.

The requirements for boys at home under a tutor would be parallel to
those which have been described; so that no separate discussion of the case
is needed; but as it is so little the custom now to keep boys at home in this
way, we may consider it quite unnecessary to provide formally for them.

Robert Kerr, *The Gentleman's House* (1865), p. 147.

'ANY ROOM IS GOOD ENOUGH FOR A SCHOOLROOM'

As Kerr's influential volume shows, the standard of schoolrooms, no less than any other room in the middle- and upper-class home, attracted attention in works of household design. But educational writers themselves saw that the material conditions of learning – the need for warmth, light and good ventilation – were crucial to the success of educational programmes, and stressed the importance of environment, a relatively new concept, in the cultivation of mind as well as body. In The English Schoolroom, *Anthony Thomson pricked the middle-class conscience by drawing attention to the appalling and hypocritical neglect of schoolrooms in houses otherwise renowned for their interior furnishings, and by suggesting that middle-class children were less well served in this respect than those of the poor.*

The rooms usually set apart as schoolrooms in houses of any pretension, and even of great pretension, are, in most instances, the very worst that can be picked out. They are mostly the dullest, the dampest, the poorest, or the most useless chambers in the whole building. 'Any room is good enough for a schoolroom' – such is the almost universal cry when arranging the accommodation of a great house; and even when such is being built, schoolrooms are about the last chambers to be considered. How much, then, it may be asked, of the idea of gloom, weariness, and wretchedness, usually connected with instruction by children of all ages and ranks, is traceable to the miserable rooms in which it is too often carried on. Take a child out of the bare-walled, bare-floored, dully-papered, dimly-lighted back-room usually devoted to the schoolroom, where tears, and headache, or at best listlessness, are the daily accompaniment of his mental toil, into his mother's warm, well-lighted cheerful boudoir, where every object is light, airy, and gay, and see how his spirits will rise, and with it his appetite for mental operations. The weary 'exercise,' the 'hard bit' of Latin, the tiresome 'long sum,' lose half their difficulties by the change, and the little mind fully *thawed*, grasps with ease what before it could but ill, if at all, appreciate. And no wonder. Light, warmth, and ventilation are all as necessary to the mental development of a child as they are to the blooming of a flower. The proof is, that the contraries of these – dimness, cold, and closeness – all react through the body on the mind and depress the mental powers, and hence become, so far, *mental tortures*, and by the cruel and wicked have been so used in every age of the world, especially as regards children, whose intuitive dread of 'the dark' is a fact well known.

Why, then, in these matters should the children of the upper classes be worse cared for than the children of the poor? Why should a parent who loudly professes that no cost shall stand in the way of the *real* education of his child too often persist in the continuance of such influences as blanch the child's cheeks while they stunt his intellect? Simply from want of consideration. In his own rooms there is everything that can cheer, warm, and even excite the mind. He forgets that what is a necessity to *him* is just as much a necessity to his child, but, of course, in a minor degree. Just as the parent must have food, so must the child; but no one in his senses would think of putting before the child the dishes and beverages of the parent: still the *foundation* must remain the same – good meat, good bread, good water. So, too, the child demands as much, if not more, than the father or mother, of light, warmth, and ventilation.

Anthony F. Thomson, *The English Schoolroom* (1865), pp. 98–100.

A FASHIONABLE SCHOOLROOM OF THE FIN DE SIÈCLE

While the governess might do much to stamp her authority on the schoolroom, she could do little to alter its basic conditions, or to imprint her own taste upon it. Emily Peart advocated making the best of things: 'make it a fixed rule to have the schoolroom always perfectly neat, and as cheerful and pleasant as possible. Of course you can do but little in this respect – you have no choice as to the room and fittings; but do the little you can, and improve what is chosen for you.' (1869, p. 27) The aesthetic features of the schoolroom, of course, reflected the tastes, priorities and pockets of parents. Lucy Lyttleton, later Lady Frederick Cavendish, described her nursery of the 1840s as shabby: it contained, for instance, 'a battered dirty red work-table with a hole in it, through which she used to poke her finger'. (Cited in Horn, 1997, p. 30) For wealthy parents with the inclination, however, manuals of interior design had plenty of fashionable ideas for the schoolroom. Jane Panton, daughter of the painter W.P. Frith, was a well-known journalist on domestic matters.

Let me urge on all mothers of families to cling to either a day nursery or a schoolroom until the children are really too old to be glad of some place where they can do actually and positively as they like; that is to say, of course, unless they like to behave like savages, but this rarely happens in a household where the little ones have been accustomed to nice surroundings, and to be treated like human beings from their cradles.

It is most important that children should be let a great deal alone, and to insure this it is perfectly necessary that some room should be set apart for their use entirely, furnished in such a way that one is not constantly obliged to be saying 'Don't do this' and 'Don't do that,' and yet in a manner that shall foster every nice taste and encourage every good habit possible; and great care should be also taken to insure sufficient sunshine, for sunshine is life and health, and a dark and sunless room often fosters a dark and sunless nature.

I should strongly advise the floor of the schoolroom to be covered with Indian matting, if expense be no object, with rugs about at intervals: this is always clean and fresh, and can be changed often. Next to Indian matting comes the stained edge to the floor so often recommended, with the nice square of Kidderminster carpet laid down over carpet felt, and edged with a woollen fringe; the best carpets of this particular make are called 'three-ply,' and are sold by the yard. [. . .] under *no* circumstances should the schoolroom be the refuge for half-worn costly carpets, which want wearing out, and yet are too shabby for the downstairs apartments. These had far better be got rid of in some sale; for an old carpet is nothing but a dust-bin on a small scale, and can never be fresh enough to put in a room where there are children.

The walls could be covered with one of the washable sanitary papers, if one can be procured in a sufficiently pretty pattern; but it is emphatically necessary that the walls should have a real dado, either of oilcloth painted some good artistic shade – four coats are necessary to eliminate the pattern – of cretonne, or matting, which is best of all. This keeps the lower part of the wall tidy always; and if the sanitary paper can be obtained in a self-colour, the plainness of this can be done away with by a good selection of pictures, than which nothing is more necessary in the schoolroom; and children had far better be plainly dressed and fed than have bad pictures provided for them, or ugly drawings only relating to their work.

In these days of cheap art there is no reason why we should be without pictures of some kind everywhere, and they should be chosen carefully, either for their beauty or for the lesson they teach. Having a positive horror of gambling, horse-racing, or betting in any shape or form myself, I cannot regard any house satisfactorily furnished without autotypes of my father's pictures of 'The Road to Ruin.'

[. . .]

The ceiling should be papered in some bright blue and white paper, and should have a good ventilator somewhere in the centre. No gas should be allowed, and light should be furnished by two good hanging lamps conveniently placed; while each child who is old enough to do its work after tea in the winter should have its own shaded Queen's reading lamp, and should be taught to keep it clean and bright for itself.

[. . .]

There should be two good cupboards in the room, which could be placed in the recesses on each side of the fireplace, should there be any; these could be simply made with shelves in the recesses and with wooden doors to fasten over them; these could be painted some self-colour to match the prevailing colour of the room, and the panels could be filled in either with the ever-useful Japanese leather paper, or be embellished by Mrs McClelland's clever brush with studies of some lovely flowers; brass handles should be added, and while one cupboard should be set apart for the governess and the schoolroom books, the other should be so arranged that, if possible, each child should have its own shelf. The top of these cupboards could form an excellent receptacle for toys and games, while some of the hanging bookshelves spoken of before could supplement the shelves should there not be room for the extra books. The windows must open top and bottom, and should have short muslin and cretonne curtains; no blinds, of course, but, should the situation be as sunny as it ought to be, outside blinds should be provided, and, furthermore, window-boxes for flowers should never be wanting; the children learn a great deal looking after them, and lessons are far less trying on a hot day if the room is kept cool by sun-blinds, while what air there is blows in over a sweet scent caused perhaps by that best of all mixtures, mignonette and ten-week stocks.

J.E. Panton, *From Kitchen to Garret: Hints for Young Householders* (1888), pp. 192–4.

CHAPTER 3

HEART-RENDING FIGURES AND HARROWING FACTS: THE PROBLEMS OF THE GOVERNESS LIFE

By the mid-century, the problems of the governess life had become proverbial. The rewards of teaching, the satisfaction of being self-supporting and the excitement of change were all outweighed in the popular imagination by the 'plight' of the lady 'reduced' to a position of precarious dependence and subservience in another woman's home. Amplified by the success in 1847 of *Jane Eyre* and *Agnes Grey*, protests in the press, in popular novels and in graphic form about the scandalous treatment of governesses 'as a class' became frequent and widespread. Feminists, philanthropists and educationalists, as well as governesses themselves, added their voices to the debate. Chapter 4 will recount some of the measures advocated and taken by these interested parties. Here, however, we focus on the allegations and appeals that turned the distress of individual governesses into a matter of national concern.

For the governess herself, the potential problems of her lot were manifold. First she had to face the opprobrium attached to middle-class women's paid work, both from members of her own social class and, in the 'hungry '40s', from men of all classes competing for ascendancy in the job market. As we have seen, the process of finding a job was fraught with hazards. If she managed to secure employment, a resident governess might suffer isolation from her friends and family – might even find herself starved of adult company altogether. Her ambiguous

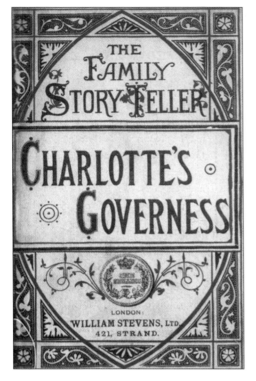

Figs 24–26 These attractive volumes, published at the turn of the century, show that in literature for young girls, the fascination of the governess figure outlived the 'governess question' by several decades.

relationship with employers who were wealthier, but often less well-educated and lower down the social scale than she, meant that she might feel out of place and compromised if invited into the family group; neglected and lonely if excluded from it. The uncertainty of her status frequently deprived her of authority over the children for whose behaviour and instruction she was responsible. The schoolroom over which she presided was prone to interruptions on the whim of her employer; even her sleeping quarters were only tenuously her own, and might be called upon if guests were expected. Resented by the servants for her supposed pretensions, distrusted as a rival by the lady of the house, she must often have felt like a pariah.

The unreasonably various, exhausting and time-consuming tasks expected of the governess were well known: ill health, depression and nervous debility seem to have been commonplace. If her hours were long, her pay was almost always meagre. Many found it difficult to 'keep up appearances', and most found it impossible to save for their old age, especially if, as seems often to have been the case, they had dependents – aged parents, siblings or even children of their own – to support. Many faced destitution upon retirement.

Daily governesses, who rushed from one set of pupils to another; finishing governesses responsible for young ladies impatient to 'come out'; specialist teachers of music, drawing and languages; governesses who opened or joined small private 'academies'; and so-called 'holiday governesses' who filled in when emergencies arose: all experienced variations on the predicament of the more familiar resident governess, while sharing with her the problems of insecurity of tenure, exploitation, and prejudice. All, furthermore, competed with and involuntarily undercut one another for the same work.

As Mary Poovey has argued, the fate of the governess represented disturbing contradictions within middle-class beliefs about class and gender. The ability to afford a governess, and to have one's daughters lavishly educated at home, was a sign of prosperity and success in genteel society. Yet affordable governesses were supplied by the failures, bankruptcies and improvidencies of the very sector of society to whom they were called to serve. At the same time, middle-class ideals of femininity called for virtuous self-sacrifice, seclusion from the stresses and temptations of the capitalist marketplace, devotion to the home, and an education tailored exclusively to the role of 'Angel in the House'. In all these respects, the professional governess cast doubt, in her own person and actions, on the very ideals she was supposed to embody.

How accurately the personal experiences and collective wishes – positive and negative – of governesses are represented by those speaking to, about and for them in the press is open to debate. Rightly or wrongly, however, their struggles smote the consciences, and continue to capture the imaginations, of generations of readers.

A HANKERING AFTER HAPPINESS

When her father's firm and the family fortune collapsed in the 1820s, Harriet Martineau was precluded by her deafness from governessing or teaching music. However, her sister did take on the role while Martineau herself attempted to make a living from teaching 'by correspondence'. The scheme failed, encouraging her to attempt – very successfully as it turned out – to make her living by her pen. She remained interested in and on the whole sympathetic towards governesses, as her only novel Deerbrook *testifies.*

'So you spend all your days alone here,' said she, looking around upon the rather bare walls, the matted floor, the children's desks, and the single shelf which held Miss Young's books.

'Not exactly all the day alone,' replied Miss Young; 'the children are with me five hours a day, and a set of pupils from the village comes to me besides, for a spare hour of the afternoon. In this way I see a good many little faces every day.'

'And some others too, I should hope; some besides little faces?'

Miss Young was silent. Margaret hastened on –

'I suppose most people would say here what is said everywhere else about the nobleness and privilege of the task of teaching children. But

I do not envy those who have it to do. I am as fond of children as any one; but then it is having them out to play on the grass, or romping with them in the nursery, that I like. When it becomes a matter of desks and school-books, I had far rather study than teach.'

'I believe everybody, except perhaps mothers, would agree with you,' said Miss Young, who was now, without apology, plying her needle.

'Indeed! then I am very sorry for you.'

'Thank you; but there's no need to be sorry for me. Do you suppose that one's comfort lies in having a choice of employments? My experience leads me to think the contrary.'

'I do not think I could be happy,' said Hester, 'to be tied down to an employment I did not like.'

'Not to a positively disgusting one. But I am disposed to think that the greatest number of happy people may be found busy in employments that they have not chosen for themselves, and never would have chosen.'

'I am afraid these very happy people are haunted by longings to be doing something else.'

'Yes: there is their great trouble. They think, till experience makes them wiser, that if they were only in another set of circumstances, if they only had a choice what they would do, a chance for the exercise of the powers they are conscious of, they would do such things as should be the wonder and the terror of the earth. But their powers may be doubted, if they do not appear in the conquest of circumstances.'

'So you conquer these giddy children, when you had rather be conquering German metaphysicians, or – , or – , what else?'

'There is little to conquer in these children,' said Miss Young; 'they are very good with me. I assure you I have much more to conquer in myself, with regard to them. It is but little that I can do for them; and that little I am apt to despise, in the vain desire to do more.'

'How more?'

'If I had them in a house by myself, to spend their whole time with me, so that I could educate, instead of merely teaching them —. But here I am doing just what we were talking of just now, – laying out a pretty-looking field of duty, in which there would probably be as many thorns as in any other. Teaching has its pleasures, – its great occasional, and small daily pleasures, though they are not to be compared to the sublime delights of education.'

'You must have some of these sublime delights mixed in with the humbler. You are, in some degree, educating these children while teaching them.'

'Yes: but it is more a negative than a positive function, a very humble one. Governesses to children at home can do little more than stand between children and the faults of the people around them. I speak quite generally.'

'Is such an occupation one in which anybody can be happy?'

'Why not, as well as in making pins' heads, or in nursing sick people, or in cutting square blocks out of a chalk pit for thirty years together, or in any other occupation which may be ordained to prove to us that happiness lies in the temper, not in the object of a pursuit? Are there not free and happy pin-makers, and sick-nurses, and chalk-cutters?'

'Yes: but they know how much to expect. They have no idea of pin-making in itself being great happiness.'

'Just so. Well: let a governess learn what to expect; set her free from a hankering after happiness in her work, and you have a happy governess.'

'I thought such a thing was out of the order of nature.'

'Not quite. There have been such, though there are strong influences against it. The expectations of all parties are unreasonable; and those who are too humble or too amiable, to be dissatisfied with others, are discontented with themselves, when the inevitable disappointment comes. There is a great deal said about the evils of the position of a governess – between the family and the servants – a great deal said that is very true, and always will be true, while governesses have proud hearts, like other people: but these are slight evils in comparison with the grand one of the common failure of the relation. – There, do you hear that bell?'

'What is it? The breakfast bell?'

'Yes. You must go. I would not be understood as inviting you here; for it is not, except upon sufferance, my room; and I have no inducement to offer. But I may just say, that you will always be welcome.'

'Always?' said Margaret. 'In and out of school hours?'

'In and out of school hours, unless your presence should chance to turn my pupils' heads. In that case, you will not be offended if I ask you to go away.'

Harriet Martineau, *Deerbrook* (first published 1839, 1983), pp. 20–2.

THE DISCOMFORTS OF A HALF-WAY PLACE

Harriet Martineau's Miss Young remains tactfully discreet about the shifts and compromises of her own situation; the reader is made painfully aware of them nevertheless. Emily Peart's volume of advice is a great deal more forthright in detailing the difficulties of the governess's position.

There is a point about which much of the discomfort and vexation respecting governesses are constantly arising – I mean their social position in the houses where they dwell. Of course there is much to be said on both sides. There are many people with a governess in their house who have not the least idea how to treat her, or of what is due to her position as a lady and an inmate of their home; and there are many many governesses so touchy and so apt to stand upon their rights, so afraid of doing anything more than they actually bargained to do, so ready to imagine slights, and so unwilling to forgive them when they are shown, that it is a real impossibility for any lady to treat them so as to give any satisfaction to either party. The position of a governess is often an extremely difficult one, and one in which tact and ready apprehension are required to steer clear of trouble. Sometimes she is made a confidante, and a recipient of family secrets; sometimes she witnesses scenes which ought never to take place; sometimes she is treated with familiarity by one head of the household, and with coldness and suspicion by the other; noticed alike with approbation and jealousy; unavoidably witnessing and hearing much which should never go beyond the family circle, she needs no little discrimination and nice feeling to go on smoothly and well. It is this very position – this

Fig. 27 A marginal and often shadowy figure, the governess might find herself a
reluctant witness to family secrets.

anomalous half-way place, which has given rise so often to what is
unpleasant, and has caused a kind of unacknowledged slur to rest on the
name of 'governess'.

[Emily Peart], *A Book for Governesses, by One of Them* (1869),
pp. 98–9.

QUIZZING THE GOVERNESS

*The peculiar position of the governess often made her feel at once
socially invisible and socially exposed. In this famous scene, the
exasperatingly eligible Hon. Blanche Ingram attempts to provoke
her host, Mr Rochester, at Jane Eyre's expense.*

M r Rochester having quitted the Eshtons, stands on the hearth as solitary as she [Blanche Ingram] stands by the table: she confronts him, taking her station at the opposite side of the mantelpiece.

'Mr Rochester, I thought you were not fond of children?'

'Nor am I.'

'Then what induced you to take charge of such a little doll as that?' (pointing to Adèle). 'Where did you pick her up?'

'I did not pick her up; she was left on my hands.'

'You should have sent her to school.'

'I could not afford it: schools are so dear.'

'Why, I suppose you have a governess for her: I saw a person with her just now – is she gone? Oh, no! There she is still, behind the window-curtain. You pay her, of course; I should think it quite as expensive – more so; for you have them both to keep in addition.'

I feared – or should I say, hoped? – the allusion to me would make Mr Rochester glance my way; and I involuntarily shrank further into the shade: but he never turned his eyes.

'I have not considered the subject,' said he indifferently, looking straight before him.

'No, you men never do consider economy and common sense. You should hear mamma on the chapter of governesses. Mary and I have had, I should think, a dozen at least in our day; half of them detestable and the rest ridiculous, and all incubi – were they not, mamma?'

'Did you speak, my own?'

The young lady thus claimed as the dowager's special property, reiterated her question with an explanation.

'My dearest, don't mention governesses; the word makes me nervous. I have suffered a martyrdom from their incompetency and caprice. I thank Heaven I have now done with them!'

Mrs Dent here bent over to the pious lady, and whispered something in her ear; I suppose, from the answer elicited, it was a reminder that one of the anathematized race was present.

'Tant pis!' said her ladyship. 'I hope it may do her good!' Then, in a lower tone, but still loud enough for me to hear, 'I noticed her; I am a judge of physiognomy, and in hers I see all the faults of her class.'

'What are they, madam?' inquired Mr Rochester aloud.

'I will tell you in your private ear,' replied she, wagging her turban three times with portentous significance.

'But my curiosity will be past its appetite; it craves food now.'

'Ask Blanche; she is nearer you than I.'

'Oh, don't refer him to me, mamma! I have just one word to say of the whole tribe; they are a nuisance. Not that I ever suffered much from them; I took care to turn the tables. What tricks Theodore and I used to play on our Miss Wilsons, and Mrs Greys, and Madame Jouberts. Mary was always too sleepy to join in a plot with spirit. The best fun was with Madame Joubert: Miss Wilson was a poor, sickly thing, lachrymose and low-spirited, not worth the trouble of vanquishing, in short; and Mrs Grey was coarse and insensible; no blow took effect on her. But poor Madame Joubert! I see her yet in her raging passions, when we had driven her to extremities – spilt our tea, crumbled our bread and butter, tossed our books up to the ceiling, and played a charivari with the ruler and desk, the fender and fire-irons. Theodore, do you remember those merry days?'

'Yaas, to be sure I do,' drawled Lord Ingram; 'and the poor old stick used to cry out, "Oh you villains childs" and then we sermonized her on the presumption of attempting to teach such clever blades as we were, when she was herself so ignorant.' [. . .]

Amy Eshton [. . .] joined in with her soft, infantine voice: 'Louisa and I used to quiz our governess too; but she was such a good creature, she would bear anything: nothing put her out. She was never cross with us; was she, Louisa?'

'No, never; we might do what we pleased – ransack her desk and her workbox, and turn her drawers inside out; and she was so good-natured, she would give us anything we asked for.'

'I suppose, now,' said Miss Ingram, curling her lips sarcastically, 'we shall have an abstract of the memoirs of all the governesses extant. In order to avert such a visitation, I again move the introduction of a new topic.'

Charlotte Brontë, *Jane Eyre* (1985, first published 1847), pp. 205–7.

SERVANTS AND GOVERNESSES: A WORD OF CAUTION

The intermediate status of the governess rendered her liable to contempt and ridicule both from above – the employer class – and below. To the servants of the house a prickly, defensive governess must have seemed fair game. The tone taken here by the ever-vigilant Emily Peart suggests something of the embarrassment suffered by governesses on this account – and at the same time betrays the attitude that could cause the trouble.

It is proverbial that servants dislike governesses, and are very unwilling to believe that there can be much good about them any way; they are very ready to see many faults in them, and to resist, from prejudice, the belief that they are ladies. Have as little to do with them as possible; treat them with invariable politeness; and see that what is right to be done for you *is* done, and then require no more. It needs simply *uninterfering* conduct on the part of a governess to disarm almost any servant, and to secure the attention which she ought to have. Never assume the least tone of authority in any way; and whatever has to be spoken about, let it be done, by all means, through the mistress. She is the proper person to see to it, not you. Let the servant who attends to you feel that you require her duties, as far as you are concerned, to be properly done, and after that you wish nothing more. The unceasing worry and unending discomfort which some ladies think it necessary to suffer on account of their servants, is something wonderful. Surely when one thinks of the unheard-of failings of servants, as ladies find them, the wonder is that any lady ever can be suited with a governess; for if a lady find it impossible to obtain a person who will perform the inferior offices of her household to her mind, how can she have much hope of finding one who will perform the higher work of educating children wisely and well? In all your intercourse with servants be a lady, and if occasion offer, be a friend; do not lose any such opportunity, should it occur, and I do not think you will have much occasion to complain of the servants. There is an innate sense of justice and honour in the heart of the poor, undulled by the

FLUNKEIANA.

Enter THOMAS, *who gives warning.*

Gentleman. "OH, CERTAINLY! YOU CAN GO, OF COURSE; BUT, AS YOU HAVE BEEN WITH ME FOR NINE YEARS, I SHOULD LIKE TO KNOW THE REASON."

Thomas. "WHY, SIR, IT'S MY *FEELINS*. YOU USED ALWAYS TO READ PRAYERS, SIR, YOURSELF—AND SINCE MISS WILKINS HAS BIN HERE, SHE BIN A READING OF 'EM. NOW I CAN'T *BEMEAN* MYSELF BY SAYIN 'AMEN' TO A GUV'NESS."

Fig. 28 Distinctions of status rankled as sorely below stairs as above. (*Punch*, 1848)

pride of riches and true to its own instinct; and they see many a thing, and feel many a truth, to which the mistress is blind and dull.

[Emily Peart], *A Book for Governesses, by One of Them* (1869), pp. 103–4.

A FACETIOUS CALL FOR ACTION

The satirical magazine Punch, *which wavered between affectionate derision of governesses and outrage at their predicament, found in the plight of these 'higher' servants of the middle classes a banner behind which its readers might unite. Conveniently enough, of course, in jokingly urging the governess to strike, the magazine also found an excuse to condemn working-class militancy.*

A Governess Strike Wanted

As striking seems infectious, we really almost wonder that the Governesses don't Strike. They have certainly more cause for it than nine-tenths of the workmen who have recently turned out. Few workmen work harder than do our poor Governesses, and clearly none receive worse wages for their work. The following advertisement will show the price of Governess-labour as last quoted in the market, and it seems to us quite low enough to justify a Strike:–

RESIDENT GOVERNESS WANTED (in the country), who is qualified to educate five children, between the ages of 5 and 14, in the English courses, with French, music, and drawing, a person above 25 years of age, and willing to look after the children's wardrobes, preferred. Salary 20 guineas per annum, with laundry expenses. Apply by letter only to J.B., — Street, Islington.

To educate a 'child' of the advanced age of fourteen in English, French, and music, to say nothing of drawing, could scarcely take less school-time than full three hours per diem. For a child of five years old, the schooling might be shorter; but the teaching of five children, aged between five and fourteen, could hardly average less than quite ten hours a day, and such hard labour has a claim upon the interest (and the capital) of people who support what is called the Nine Hours Movement.

The offered wages for this work are one-and-twenty pounds per annum, which is about the same as that of upper housemaids and head cooks. Such pay is at the rate of not one penny more than eight shillings a week; dividing this by five, we ascertain that one-and-seven pence is the precise cost to the parents of each child's daily schooling. In making out this reckoning, we omit to count the cost of the residence and washing; for we look upon these items as the wages which are offered for the work of 'looking after' what the writer calls the 'wardrobes', but which, using plainer language, we should call the children's 'clothes'. To teach 'the English courses' (whatever they may be), a Governess, of course, must be well versed in English; but we think, however closely she may look into her Dictionary, she will not learn from it the meaning of the verb active 'to look after', as it is used in the advertisement which offers her a place. To 'look after', in the sense in which the advertiser uses it, means certainly to 'mend', and probably to 'make'. So that the 'person' who is said to be wanted as a Governess, will find the post of sempstress really is her place.

To conclude as we began. We have, in general, we own, no sympathy with Strikes, and except in extreme cases, we should never recommend them. Men who try by striking to better their condition find it turns out *'wice worsa'*, and that, for the most part, their turns-out make it worse. But the position of our Governesses is really now so bad, that almost any change would better it; and were a Governess Strike to be attempted, we think some striking benefit might possibly result.

'A Governess Strike Wanted', *Punch* (3 September 1859), p. 96.

MONEY MATTERS

Comparing and contrasting the rights – and sufferings – of middle-class governesses and the working-class poor was a consistent feature of the debate, almost always to the advantage of the governesses. In this early article on the subject from Fraser's Magazine, *Lady Eastlake insists not only that the governess lacks the welfare safety nets (arguably) available to the 'lower classes', but also that, with her refined and educated sensibility, she will feel her poverty more keenly.*

This brings us to the *£.s.d.* part of the business. Very shameful instances of insufficient payment for hard service might be adduced. We rather wish, by taking the average, to secure ourselves from the charge of exaggeration. Every one is too willing to silence his own conscience by impeaching his neighbour's. We hope we may be deemed to strike the mean, if we fix the usual rate of payment at 35*l.* per annum. We believe that where there is one at 40*l.* there are two at 30*l.* Many receive much higher salaries. 100*l.* per annum may be the maximum. We know that 12*l.* per annum has been offered and accepted. If our average be incorrect, a philanthropist could scarcely do a greater service to society than by furnishing an accurate paper of statistics on the subject. Dr Kitchener, when he wished to prove that servants' wages were too low, specified each item of their wants. Let us do the same for governesses:–

	£	s	d
Dress	16	0	0
Washing	6	0	0
Postage and stationery	3	0	0
Casualties	2	0	0
	27	0	0

The sum total of specified expenses subtracted from a yearly income of 35*l.* leaves 8*l.* per annum to lay by for old age. Even from this remainder must be deducted the probable charge for doctors' bills and journeys. Where the salary is higher, we may reasonably believe the governess's outlay must be greater, especially when we reflect that many ladies expect their governesses to dress expensively, for the credit of the house, as they think. Now, what is to become of those women who, after toiling out the best of their days, survive to old age? How are they to subsist? What means of maintenance are available to women sixty years of age? Is it just that the work of youth should not exempt age from want? The lower classes have clubs, poor-laws and unions – rough roadsteads, surely, for that last anchorage. But the superannuated governess has not even these. There must be many aged or broken-down women suffering hourly such destitution as the lowest class cannot feel, whilst the state protects them. It is those who have known better days, and have a decent appearance to keep up, who gnaw the lip in silence, and die without appeal. Thank God, some hearts have at last been moved to make a fund for disabled governesses. This is not enough: this is giving alms where alms should not be needed, except in particular cases of distress. Every one who has the power ought to be able, through his industry, to maintain himself. We have sometimes been astonished at comparing the qualifications required in letters of inquiry touching governesses with the remuneration offered, – such a catalogue of literary, ornamental, and moral acquirements as one would think no ordinary mortal would lay claim to; and all these demands on body and mind to be paid by a paltry 40*l.* a-year! It is not a fair interest upon the capital invested in the girl's education. One cannot learn French, German, Italian, Latin, music, dancing, and drawing, to say nothing of history, globes and arithmetic, for nothing. It may be asked, Why does the girl close with such an offer? Let the old proverb reply, 'Better half a loaf than no bread'. The market is over-stocked; governesses are much at a discount. Many ladies would not dare to treat their maids as they behave to the teacher of their children. Why? The maid has a broad field before her; she can afford to turn upon her mistress. The governess must endure all things or perish. A low marriage or a slow death are her only loopholes of escape. Oh, shame on us who make a gain of the pressing miseries of others!

[Lady Eastlake], 'Hints on the Modern Governess System'
(30 November, 1844), pp. 577–8.

DAILY GOVERNESSES

In default of reliable statistics as Lady Eastlake noted, anecdotal evidence accumulated in the press. The letters page of The Times, *in particular, provided a forum for a variety of grievances, the correspondents often commenting on and replying to each other's allegations.*

To the Editor of The Times

Sir, – I hope you will permit me to say a word on this subject. I was very much surprised to see by the letter of 'A Constant Reader' how little is known of the pay usually received by daily governesses. I can assure him for a fact that I was offered 5s. a week by a lady 'living not a hundred miles' from Harley-Street, Cavendish-square, to teach her four children – the eldest a girl of 14 – the usual accomplishments taught by governesses, as well as the rudiments of Latin to two boys; the hours to be from half-past 9 o'clock to 5. I was, it is true, to be allowed to dine at half-past 1 o'clock with my pupils. I felt that while there was a crossing to sweep I could not accept the lady's offer, as while attending her children I would be expected to appear well dressed, while, if I followed the occupation of crossing-sweeper, I should probably acquire more means of being well-dressed, and not needing to be so, might put by my earnings till sickness might come upon me. Another lady, also living in a fashionable neighbourhood, offered me two pounds a year to attend her three children, hours from 10 till 3. A quarter's notice to be given on either side. This 'eligible offer' I also felt myself compelled to refuse. I could tell of twenty such instances – indeed, I am sorry to see how little is known on the subject of the teachers of the future generation. I will venture to say that nine out of ten daily governesses will consider the paltry sum offered by the lady your correspondent speaks of as much above the average amount of pay received by them. There is at this moment a young lady, whose education was received at a first-rate school, anxiously looking for employment as a daily governess, who has been told her demand of 'four pounds' a quarter is a great deal too much, and that by people who are paying their cooks 30 guineas a year. I and others I could name have frequently regretted our fates, to be, as we are, daughters of gentlemen, well-educated, and obliged to keep an appearance often upon half the sum received by our sisters in the kitchen, who are not expected to keep up any appearance at all.

> I remain, Sir, yours most respectfully,
> ONE WHO HAS SEEN SOME DARK SHADOWS
> May 6.

'Daily Governesses', *The Times* (8 May 1852), p. 8.

Managing Mothers

A further source of anxiety lay in the governess's often trying, and almost always contradictory, relationship with the mother of her charges. Although the two roles overlapped in important ways, they were often at odds with each other both in theory and practice. Emily Peart catalogued a wide variety of irritating mothers for whom the prospective governess should be prepared: jealous mothers, weak mothers, interfering mothers, tyrannical and overbearing mothers. Paradoxically, she admitted, the easiest mother to deal with from the professional educator's point of view was the worst one from the world's: the woman who handed over the care of her children – that most sacred of duties – entirely to her governess. There were, however, many other types . . .

But there is another kind of mother you may have to deal with – the ideal of what a woman should be in one way, – so sweet, so loving, so amiable, so unspeakably graceful and winning that it were impossible to help loving her; while, at the same time, you cannot shut your eyes to the fact of her utter inefficiency in the management of her children, and her arrangements for you; so obliging – that there is not a thing you might ask for which she would not at once promise you might have, and yet so lacking energy that she never obtains it for you; so accommodating, that she will agree to every plan, and think all you wish to do is just the best thing that could be done; but you never find one plan a particle nearer completion, because she never thinks anything more about it; and she is so sweet and amiable you don't like to trouble her, or be ever 'at her'; so placid and graceful, that the greatest irregularity, the most irritating disorder, never puts her the least out of the way, and therefore never gets rectified; so fond of her children, that the most flagrant disobedience never elicits more than, 'Oh, you really are very naughty'; so fascinating, that she looks well even in a house dirty and untidy, with children disobedient and rude, and servants neglectful and impertinent; so winning, that though you are irritated and provoked by her beyond endurance, you cannot help loving her, and thinking there is no one else like her. And yet such a woman is most trying to any one who really loves order and good habits: she makes those around her vexed and irritated; her children see her weakness, and her servants secretly despise her; for, however fascinating any one may be, wrong-doing cannot procure respect. If you have to do with such a woman, make up your mind to one thing – never be irritated and vexed at her; thoroughly understand her; do not expect anything from her; accept her sweetness, enjoy her amiability, and go steadily and quietly on in your own duties; when they come into contact with her, make them to clash as lightly as possible, and do not be influenced by her one way or another. Such people are certainly trying, because it is impossible to be vexed with them, however vexatious they are; and it is hard work for a governess to make children orderly and obedient and industrious, when all the influence around is exactly in an opposite direction. How is it possible for her to win children from habits, when they are constantly saying, 'Well, but mamma always lets us do so'; 'Mamma says nothing to us'; 'Why, mamma did so yesterday?'

[Emily Peart], *A Book for Governesses, by One of Them* (1869),
pp. 137–9.

EXPLOITATION IN THE SUBURBS

Though exempted from the problems of rivalry with mothers, the governess in a private academy, often based in the proprietor's home, shared many of the practical and material – if not the social – inconveniences of domestic governessing. And the wages, likewise, were often criminally low.

To the Editor of The Times

Sir, – Many distressing cases of the want of humanity displayed by those engaging governesses in schools and private families have lately appeared in your paper; but one unparalleled in the heartrending catalogue of those who grind down female talent and industry to the lowest level, debasing it in the very dust, and causing the unhappy victims to rue the day they were born, lately came under my notice, which I shall be obliged by your inserting in your journal. A young lady lately applied for the situation of teacher in a school in one of our suburbs; music, French, and the usual routine of an English education were required of her; ten weeks of the year (during the different holydays) she was told she must board and lodge herself, her washing she must likewise pay, and in return a salary of 10*l.* was offered, with the additional information, that she must consider herself well off, for that the last teacher had only 8*l.*! 'Can such things be, and come over us like a summer cloud, without our special wonder!' I need not comment on this 'o'er true tale,' its glaring inhumanity and injustice plead for themselves.

I am, Sir, your obedient servant,

A SISTER.

Notting-hill, Oct. 26

To the Editor, *The Times* (28 October 1844), p. 8.

HOW CAN I TAKE A HOLIDAY?

Like the 'well-off' teacher above, the resident governess often found that holidays were arranged in spite of, rather than for her. This novel for girls shows that the problem of managing one's own time was still an emotive one in the early twentieth century.

A footman entered and summoned her to Lady Lydley's presence. 'Her Ladyship,' he said, 'would be glad if Miss Stanley would come up to her dressing-room. She wished to speak to her before she went out.'

'What a wonder,' said Agatha to herself, 'she is actually going to give me notice of our future movements.'

She took her way upstairs, and knocked at the door of Lady Lydley's dressing-room, recalling as she did so her first and only visit there; and thinking how much she had experienced since, and how long ago it seemed.

'Come in,' said Lady Lydley's voice from within.

Agatha entered, half expecting to see Lady Lydley sitting at her dressing-table, wrestling with the refractory curl.

But the tableau was a different one this time.

She was reclining on the sofa in a magnificent and most becoming 'peignoir' reading a French novel.

'Oh, there you are, Miss Stanley,' she said, putting down her book: 'Sit down, won't you. I wanted to speak to you about your holiday.'

'My holiday!' repeated Agatha, perplexed.

'Yes, your summer holiday. You can take it when we go down to Lydley, and you can have five weeks or even longer if you like.'

'But I don't want a holiday!' exclaimed Agatha, 'I never dreamt of asking for one.'

Lady Lydley gave a light laugh.

'That is very good of you,' she said, 'and very unlike many of the governesses of the day, who sometimes insist upon Easter and Christmas as well as the summer. But in this instance it will be a mutual advantage; as we shall be very full at Lydley for the first few weeks after going down there, and shall want every room we can muster. So that it will really be a convenience.'

Agatha for once was taken off her guard, and in the stress of the moment exclaimed in an almost panic-stricken manner:

'But . . . but . . . I have no home to go to. My father is at sea, and my home is broken up. How can I take a holiday?'

There was a pause. Any one but Lady Lydley would have been touched at the sight of her evident distress. But she had no womanly feeling for the forlorn and pretty girl she was turning out of her house on so short a notice.

'I am sorry,' she said, 'but as I said before we want the rooms. You surely must have some friends,' she added rather irritably, 'who would take you in! Or are there no governesses' homes or places of that kind you could go to?'

Agatha's pride now came to her assistance, and by an effort she regained her self-control. Come what might, she felt she would not allow Lady Lydley to know how entirely forlorn her position was. It came to her mind too, with a flash, that there were such posts as 'Holiday Governesses' to be had at this time of year.

Drawing herself up to her full height, her colour rising, 'I will at once make some arrangements,' she said, 'and shall be ready to go whenever it suits you.'

But she was thankful that the children were not in the schoolroom when she returned to it.

For, now that there was no longer any need to keep up a bold front, her pride all ebbed away, and she sank down in a chair, feeling utterly forlorn and miserable.

What was she to do! What would her father say to her leaving the place he had settled her in! But she had no choice. She was simply turned out of the house. How, even if there were such posts to be had as those of 'holiday governesses', was she to hear of a suitable one? How could she trust to an advertisement! What would he say if she did such a thing?

Florence Montgomery, *Behind the Scenes in the Schoolroom* (1913), pp. 178–81.

TOO HIGH FOR THE KITCHEN, TOO LOW FOR THE PARLOUR

A generation of popular novelists found the sufferings of the governess irresistible as a source of pathos and melodrama. Every aspect of her life seemed fraught with anxiety: where should she sit in the carriage? Should she announce herself at the door with the double knock of a lady, or ring down to the servants' hall? In Mrs Hall's story of 1858, The Governess, *we witness a familiar set of images congealing into a cliché.*

'Pschaw, lady!' interrupted the strange old man; 'no words about it. I have not been so long your opposite neighbour without knowing that your last governess did not sit at your table; that when you had the hot, she had the cold; that when a visitor came, she went; that she was treated as a creature belonging to an intermediate state of society, which has never been defined or illustrated – being too high for the kitchen, too low for the parlour; that she was to govern her temper towards those who never governed their tempers towards her; that she was to cultivate intellect, yet sit silent as a fool; that she was to instruct in all accomplishments, which she must know and feel, yet never play anything in society except quadrilles, *because* she played so well that she might eclipse the young ladies who, not being governesses, play for husbands, while she only plays for bread! My good madam, I know almost every governess who enters Kensington by sight; the daily ones by their early hours, cotton umbrellas, and the cowed, dejected air with which they raise the knocker, uncertain how to let it fall. Do I not know the musical ones by the worn-out boa doubled round their throats, and the roll of new music clasped in the thinly-gloved hand? and the drawing ones – God help them! by the small portfolio, pallid cheeks, and haggard eyes? I could tell you tales of those hard-labouring classes that would make factory labour seem a toy; but you would not understand me. . . .'

Mrs S.C. Hall, *The Governess: A Tale* (1858), pp. 21–2.

THE HARVEST OF GOVERNESSES

Few commentators saw past the litany of personal tragedies to the structural contradictions at the heart of the Governess Question. One of the few was Lady Eastlake, who, in an early review of two governess novels, anticipated one of the ideological blindspots in the debate as a whole.

If these times puzzle us how to meet the claims and wants of the lower classes of our dependants, they puzzle and shame us too in the case of that highest dependant of all, the governess – who is not only entitled to our gratitude and respect by her position, but, in nine cases out of ten, by the circumstances which reduced her to it. For the case of the governess is so much the harder than that of any other class of the community, in that they are not only quite as liable to all the vicissitudes of life, but are absolutely supplied by them. There may be, and are, exceptions to this rule, but the real definition of a governess in the English sense, is a being who is our equal in birth, manners and education, but our inferior in worldly wealth. Take a lady, in every meaning of the word, born and bred, and let her father pass through the gazette, and she wants nothing more to suit our highest *beau idéal* of a guide and instructress to our children. We need the imprudencies, extravagancies, mistakes, or crimes of a certain number of fathers, to sow that seed from which we reap the harvest of governesses. There is no other class of labourers for hire who are thus systematically supplied by the misfortunes of our fellow creatures. There is no other class which so cruelly requires its members to be, in birth, mind, and manners, above their station, in order to fit them for their station.

[Lady Eastlake], '*Vanity Fair, Jane Eyre* and the Governesses Benevolent Institution' (1848), pp. 176–7.

PROFESSIONALLY PENSIVE

Repetitive and sometimes sentimental, the iconography of the governess's predicament helped to raise social awareness of the problem even as it obscured important issues and conflicting evidence. In Jean Ingelow's delightful short story, the heroine Ann Salters, a girl from unpretentious farming stock who has been brought up to be a governess, falls foul, not of the problems of her role, but of the imagery associated with it.

Doctor Deane's Governess

I do not like this title. It should have been 'Dr Deane's Children's Governess'; but that sounds awkward, and we English are fond of clipping out all words that are not uttered with ease. We never say, Mrs Richardson's Children's Governess, or Mrs Chichester's Children's Governess, – so let it be Dr Deane's Governess, it will save trouble.

Dr Deane's governess, Miss Ann Salter, was quietly seated, about three o'clock on a Wednesday afternoon, by the window of a pleasant little carpeted room, which was evidently used as a schoolroom. The sun shone in at the window; the light air was blowing in a good many petals of China roses. Four children were playing outside, three girls and a boy, the latter about six years old, and the girls all older. Miss Ann Salter had a book in her hands; and I can put you in possession of her attitude at once, if you have ever seen a pretty print called 'The Governess,' by saying that precisely and exactly in the position of 'The Governess,' sat Miss Ann Salter. If you wish to know whether she had seen the print in question, I am happy to inform you (it being my desire to oblige you with all proper information) that she had.

But if you yourself have not seen this print, I must tell you that it represents a very pretty pensive-looking girl, sitting quite alone, with her feet upon a stool, her hands dropped on her knees, and an open letter in them. Her hair is drawn in a braid from her cheek, and one

Fig. 29 Richard Redgrave's classic portrayal of 'The Poor Teacher' existed in many versions and was the basis of a popular engraving.

121

long curl falls on her neck. She is dressed in deep mourning, and is evidently musing over this letter from home; perhaps it is from a bereaved mother. There are globes in her room, and slates and maps, and children's dogs'-eared books; so there are in the room where Miss Ann Salter sits. But she is not in mourning. She is dressed in a gown of a light-brown colour, with three flounces, a stripe of blue at the edge of each, and a very pretty collar and cuffs of her own work. It is always best to be particular in describing these little matters, because it prevents mistakes.

The hands and feet represented in the print are unnaturally small. Miss Ann Salter's, however, were of the usual dimensions; her hair, dressed exactly like that of 'The Governess', was smooth, abundant and of a somewhat sandy hue. She had very light eyebrows and eyelashes, and her face, young, healthy, and plump as it was, had no pretensions to beauty, or even to good looks, excepting when she was laughing or looking very animated; then it was a pleasant young face enough, and as fresh as a milk-maid's.

At the time of which we speak her face was very gently pensive, though it was a half-holiday, though she had a new book on her lap, and though it was quarter-day.

[. . .]

[*Fanny, one of Miss Salter's pupils, tries to explain to her guardian the reason for her governess's pensive air:*]

'I have read a good many interesting stories,' said Fanny, hesitating, 'that had a governess for their heroine. The last I read was particularly interesting, and it made me feel that, as a class, they deserved a great deal of consideration, and – I don't exactly know how to say what I mean, but when I came here I felt that I ought to be particularly polite and friendly to Miss Salter, and to feel a great deal of pity for her.'

'Humph! now give me a sketch of the story.'

'Oh, the heroine is a tall, dark-eyed, lovely creature, brought up in the greatest luxury, and accustomed to associate with refined people. Her father loses all his property, and dies. The story opens with her taking leave of her bereaved mother. They are so poor that she is obliged to take her long journey in the depth of winter, on the top of a coach, and she reaches her first place at night. And the story goes on to say that the people are very vulgar, and treat her with the greatest insolence and harshness, particularly the master of the house, who dislikes her from the first.'

'But she, no doubt, is a miracle of patience and discretion?'

'Yes, uncle, she is very unhappy, but bears all with the sweetest meekness, though she often retires to her own room to weep, and think over the happy past; and then it goes on to say that she saves one of the children's lives, and the house is just going to be robbed, but she overhears the thieves talking and disclosing their plans behind a hedge.'

'A likely incident!' Well, go on.'

'It ends not quite so naturally as it begins. She marries' —

'Of course she does! The eldest son lives at home. He is a paragon of elegance and excellence, in spite of his vulgar bringing up. He is also particularly handsome; she marries him.'

'Nothing of the sort, uncle.'

'Then she marries the curate; I know she marries the curate! and immediately after, his rich uncle comes from India, lives with them, dies blessing them, and leaves them all his fortune.'

'No, she doesn't, uncle. She marries a young baronet, who is struck with the pensive sweetness of her face, as she takes the children out for a walk.'

'Indeed!'

'But the most interesting part of the story is her journal,' proceeded Fanny, 'with the description of all her lonely feelings; really it is quite harrowing to read it, – such beautiful resignation, and, at the same time, such melancholy.'

'Pray, my dear, have you talked over this story, and especially this journal, with Miss Salter?'

Jean Ingelow, *Studies for Stories* (1864), pp. 151–3, 166–8.

C H A P T E R   4

BENEVOLENCE

Graphically described in a whole spectrum of publications, the governess's lot could not fail to engender public sympathy and a certain chivalric desire to act on her behalf. Many of the governess's inconveniences were, of course, the result of her own or her employer's peculiarities, and were thus impervious to external intervention. It was in the wider circumstances of the governess life, in the securing of employment, and in provision for sickness and old age, for example, that reformers could play a part. Many of the initiatives discussed in this chapter were directed at those governesses who, for one reason or another, found themselves unemployed, unable to rely on the casual assistance of friends or relations and forced to turn to charity to survive.

Concern in the 1840s for the conditions of the poor could hardly bypass the pitiful figure of the governess, yet the path forward was not easy to discern. Administrative measures, such as the institution of workhouses for the destitute, were considered entirely inappropriate for the genteel governess, whose symbolic function would be threatened by such public forms of assistance. Middle-class reformers had much invested in securing more discreet and private means of succour for the governess. In supporting benevolent activities that firmly differentiated her from other working women and that underlined the dignity of the profession, they indirectly helped to preserve their own middle-class identity. Moreover, pervading much of the benevolence directed toward the governess was an ideology of self-discipline. The figure of the governess promulgated by reformers was never helpless, idle and eager for handouts, but hard working, accustomed to self-reliance and willing to help herself.

Though the Governesses' Mutual Assurance Society had aimed from as early as 1829 to make funds available to governesses, the first truly successful body to work on their behalf was not fully launched until 1843. Under the guidance of its Hon. Secretary, the Rev David Laing, the Governesses' Benevolent Institution (GBI) sought to 'raise the character of Governesses as a class, and thus improve the tone of Female Education; to assist Governesses in making provision for their old age; and to assist in distress and age those Governesses whose exertions for their parents, or families have prevented such a provision' (*The Story of the Governesses' Benevolent Institution*, 1962, p. 14) The backbone of the institution was to be the patronage of its wealthy subscribers, rising from 600 in 1844 to 6,000 in 1860. The society, though run by men, owed much to female support. In particular, it attracted much interest among aristocratic ladies, who saw in its activities ample opportunity for the exercise of their own philanthropic ambitions. A large proportion of the funds raised by the society was generated by activities traditionally associated with upper and middle-class femininity: a fancy sale to fund the Asylum for Aged Governesses, for example, and relentless letter writing and petitions to potential donors.

In its early days the aims of the GBI were modest, primarily involving the distribution of annuities collected from subscribers and from governesses themselves. Ten years later, however, in language which accentuated the genteel nature of the service, an advertisement in a specialized magazine for governesses attested to the variety of services offered by the society. The high standing enjoyed by the institution at this point is reflected in its list of Royal and noble patrons.

GOVERNESSES' BENEVOLENT INSTITUTION, INCORPORATED BY ROYAL
CHARTER, with power to hold freehold. Under the patronage of

Her Most Gracious Majesty.
HRH Prince Albert.
HRH the Duchess of Gloucester.

HRH the Duchess of Kent.
HRH the Duchess of Cambridge.
HRH the Duke of Cambridge.
HRH the Hereditary Grand Duchess
of Mecklenburg Strelitz.
HRH the Princess Mary Adelaide.

The objects of this Society are all in operation.

Temporary assistance to governesses in distress afforded privately and delicately through the Ladies' Committee.

Annuity Fund. – Elective annuities to aged governesses secured on invested capital, and thus independent of the prosperity of the Institution

A lady of rank has most kindly opened a fund to raise all the Society's annuities to 20*l.*, and has already received 1,900*l.* towards this desirable object. Any donations which may be kindly given may be addressed to the care of the Secretary.

Provident Fund. – Provident annuities purchased by ladies in any way connected with education, upon Government security, agreeably to the Act of Parliament. This branch includes a savings bank.

The Government allow foreign governesses to contract for these annuities.

A Home for Governesses during the intervals between their engagements.

A System of Registration, entirely free of expense.

An Asylum for the Aged.

Treasurer. – B. Bond Cabbell, Esq., M.P., F.R.S., F.S.A.

Hon. Secretary. – The Rev David Laing, M.A., F.R.S.

Bankers. – Sir S. Scott and Co., 1, Cavendish Square; Messrs. Strahan and Co., Temple Bar.

Secretary. – Charles William Klugh, Esq., at the office, 32, Sackville Street.

Advertisement, *The Governess: A Repertory of Female Education* (June 1855), p. 5.

A Home for the Disengaged

The governess was, almost by definition, likely to have few financial or familial resources to fall back on in periods of unemployment. Meagre salaries, moreover, made for small savings. From 1845, the keenest priority of the GBI was to provide a haven for those who were out of work. While the Home provided food, shelter and medical attention at low prices, it was advertised very firmly as a temporary abode, available to governesses only until they found another post. As with all the activities of the Institution, the annual report of the society lost no time in urging its committee to engage more funds.

The clerical and medical professions know but too well how many Governesses are destitute of a protector and a Home; and how the anxiety during a period of non-engagement tends as much to impair the energies, as the expense of such a time conduces to a final time of destitution. This House is intended simply as a Home – for the disengaged and unprotected; not for those, who have friends to receive and support them; not for those who wish to spend in inactivity their more active years. That the privilege may not be abused, the time of residence is strictly limited; and the weekly payment has been fixed by experienced Governesses at about half the usual cost of board and lodging. That the admissions may be carefully controlled, and that the Home may be well and economically governed, it has been placed under the care of a separate Committee of Ladies, including two of rank, not better known for their position in society, than for their clearness of intellect, their ready comprehension of business details, and their active and enlightened benevolence.

During the six months since the Home was opened, 52 Governesses have been inmates; and, as their reports of its comforts and advantages extend, the applications will rapidly increase. The benefits to the residents, are far beyond the respectability and economy of the temporary Home: the proximity of the Books of Registration affords an early opportunity for re-engagement; whilst the Honorary Surgeon, Mr

Howlett, with a zeal and kindness which the Committee have deep pleasure in acknowledging, watches over the worn labourers during their brief rest, and prepares them for fresh duties.

It is hoped, that the Home will be self-supporting; but this first year cannot but bring a heavy pressure upon the funds, notwithstanding the kind assistance of many friends. The expenses of the Lease and Furnishing have been, of course, serious; whilst the cost of management is proportionably large, until the number of inmates shall be permanently established. The balance-sheet will show how inadequate the donations have been to meet this branch of the expenditure; and how anxious the Committee must be, that other kind friends should aid them in this really important work.

Governesses' Benevolent Institution, *Annual Reports* (1846, published 1847; vol. 1, No. 6.)

A SYSTEM OF REGISTRATION FREE OF EXPENSE

The GBI was only too aware of the dangers and difficulties that could befall unsuspecting governesses in their pursuit of employment. To help avert such problems, a register for governesses and employers was established, by which both parties might benefit.

Any Governess, on procuring and leaving two satisfactory letters from respectable parties, may enter her name and such other particulars as she may wish to state. There is, also, a Book to Register applications for Governesses.

The Committee wish it to be understood, that they abstain from all interference between the parties; and that, therefore, all entries must be made by the parties themselves – Ladies in the country acting by a friend.

The Office is open from Twelve till Five.

Governesses' Benevolent Institution, *Annual Reports* (1846, published 1847), p. 2.

A Shelter for the Weather-tried Traveller

Of course, not all the governesses who approached the society for help were capable of resuming employment. Applications for annuities exposed the dire straits in which many found themselves. In 1845, the needs of a very small number of older and sick governesses were met by the building of an 'asylum' in Kentish Town, funded in part by the proceeds of an extravagant two-day Fancy Sale held in the grounds of Chelsea Hospital. To provide a permanent refuge for this sorry group of dispossessed ladies was peculiarly gratifying, as the society recognised in its early appeals for subscriptions: 'let us give her *a home who has influenced the domestic character of so many houses.'*

There is something inexpressibly sweet in the idea of providing a haven for the storm-beaten mariner – a shelter for the weather-tried traveller – a place of rest for the wearied wayfarer.

Fig. 30 The Home in Kentish Town.

The Committee have been repeatedly urged by some of their best and kindest friends to carry out the plan of a permanent Home for Aged Governesses; but they waited for the manifestation of a similar feeling on behalf of the public, in the form of donations for this especial purpose, and they have not waited in vain. Many liberal donors have come forward; and with the assistance of a highly patronised Fancy Sale at Chelsea Hospital, a sufficient sum has been accumulated to commence the Asylum with apartments for ten inmates; four of whom were elected during the past year, and four will be elected in the present year.

The necessity of such a Home is more and more pressed upon them. It seems almost superfluous again to point out how impossible it is, That Governesses in general should save sufficient to provide for their old age: A reference to one Polling Paper will be the best course, as it will produce FACTS, which are always the soundest arguments. There were Eighty-four Candidates for Three Annuities of £15 each – EIGHTY-FOUR ladies, many reared in affluence and all accustomed to the comforts and luxuries of at least our middle ranks – all seeking an Annuity of £15! Of these seventy were unmarried, and out of this number seven had incomes above £20 – two derived from Public Institutions; sixteen had incomes varying from THIRTY-SIX SHILLINGS to £14; and FORTY SEVEN had absolutely NOTHING! It will be recollected, that all these Ladies are above Fifty Years of age; and of the utterly destitute, eighteen were above Sixty. It is sometimes asked, could they not have averted this lamentable condition? The Committee would fain hope that all who have received a polling paper have read the cases to which they refer; to see that out of these seventy Ladies, no less than fifty-four had not provided for themselves, because they had devoted their salaries or their savings, legacies from relations, and all their earnings, more or less, to their families; from the 'support of one or both parents for many years,' to the educating younger sisters – helping brothers in their onward path – and protecting and educating orphan nephews and nieces. To all interested in the subject, to all who have benefited by the Governess' care, [and who has not?] it seems a duty and a privilege to provide a

Home for the desolate old age of those, whose high sense of private duty has [. . .] deprived them of a self-provided home. We cannot give them the best blessings that are conveyed in that almost sacred word; we cannot surround them with the family ties and the sweet sympathies of Home, but we CAN take them from a cheerless lodging, and the anxieties of daily privation, and the harshness of petty creditors – the half-spread table – the *not half*-warmed room – the lonely hours of increasing helplessness; and give them warmth, and food, and care, and kindness – freedom from the cruel anxiety of rent – a hand to help, a voice to cheer – the blessed certainty that their weakness will be tended – their infirmities cared for – their last days allowed to pass undisturbed by the harassing anxieties of poverty.

Governesses' Benevolent Institution, *Annual Reports* (1848, published 1849), n.p.

THE AGONIES OF THE WOULD-BE ANNUITANT

Unsurprisingly, demand for places at the asylum far exceeded its capacity, but alternative methods of help were available. In keeping with its aim of alleviating dependency, the GBI set up, almost from its inception, a Provident Fund in which governesses might invest a little of their earnings for their own use in their old age. For those already too old to work, the system of annuities – a kind of pension – was instituted. The case histories of those requesting annuities, outlined in the annual reports of the society and reproduced time and again in the national press, form a catalogue of misery and disaster as poignant as anything to be found in the novels of governess life.

MISS LOUISA B., aged 56. A Governess from 1812 to 1834, when she was disabled by paralysis, of which she has had two strokes since, and is incapable of employing herself, even with a needle. Her whole income is derived from casual assistance, having no certain support, and no relations living. – [since deceased.] *May,* 1846.

MISS ELIZABETH G., aged 51. Became a Governess at 17 in consequence of the embarrassment of her father's affairs. In conjunction with a sister, she supported her mother during 14 years, and educated three younger sisters (who are now Governesses), and a brother. The effects of influenza, gout, and inflammatory rheumatism, have for some years made her incapable even of supporting herself, and she is now without a home, and with an income of little more than £6. *May, 1846.*

MRS ARABELLA H., aged 69. Became a Governess on being left a widow at four-and-twenty, and has ever since been engaged in tuition, but has been entirely ruined by bad debts, and the dishonesty of her Solicitor, who absconded with £1200. Her advanced age prevents her gaining any employment, her health is giving way under her trials and privations, and she has no income whatever. *Nov., 1846.*

[. . .]

MISS MARY ANNE G., aged 57. Father held confidential offices in the Royal and other Scientific Societies. Left destitute by his death – Governess for many years. Obliged to relinquish her profession through deafness, and a nervous affection of the throat through fatigue in teaching. Unable to save in consequence of many deaths in her family, attended by long and afflicting illness. Two elder sisters equally destitute. Total income £3. *Nov., 1846.*

Governesses' Benevolent Institution, *Annual Reports* (1852, published 1853), n.p.

THE CASE OF MISS JANE CHERRY YOUNG

Such were the numbers of governesses applying for annuities and so evidently worthy their cases that the task of selecting the most deserving was no easy matter. To facilitate the procedure, the GBI held regular elections for which donors could purchase votes to support particular candidates. Charles Dickens was appalled on one of his frequent visits to the Society in September 1847 to find the candidates appealing for his vote in person: 'My objection to the Governesses Institution is increased every year. I think that [sic] canvassing, one of the social vices of this time: and am ashamed of possessing a vote, when I find so many reduced ladies driven to the necessity of seeking it in vain. It appears to me that there is an amount of degradation and humiliating solicitation imposed upon the candidates which is very poorly paid for, even in a successful instance, and which we are not justified in inflicting upon any class of persons, however willing they may be to undergo it.' (The Story of the Governesses' Benevolent Institution, 1962, p. 37)

Such objections ensured that public electioneering gradually disappeared, but the process of canvassing continued more discreetly by post. A card would be printed detailing an individual case which would then be circulated, usually by a sponsor, to possible voters. Miss Jane Cherry Young's case caught the attention of Christina Rossetti, who embarked upon the task of securing votes from other subscribers. Rossetti's correspondence with her former neighbour Madame Lega-Fletcher reveals something of the time and energy invested by prominent women in the workings of the society, while also charting Miss Young's frustratingly slow progress towards an annuity.

30 Torrington Square, W.C.
December 1. 1883

Dear Madam

I hope you will recollect me as more or less of a neighbour and slight acquaintance many years ago. Seeing your name in the Subscribers' List of the Governesses Benevolent Institution I venture to send you a card in case your vote and interest should not be pre-engaged. I know Miss Young's to be a genuine case worthy of sympathy and help: and tho' the May election is still a good way off, one can scarcely perhaps begin too early a canvass.

Pray allow me to remain
Very sincerely yours
Christina G. Rossetti

*   *   *

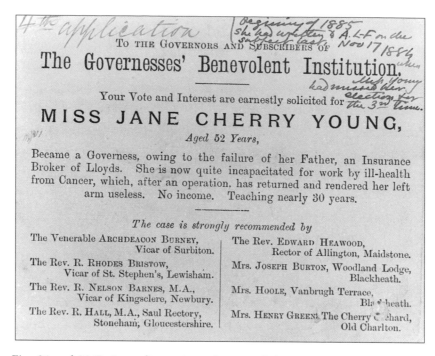

Figs 31 and 32 Eminent figures in society put their name to campaigns to help governesses in distress.

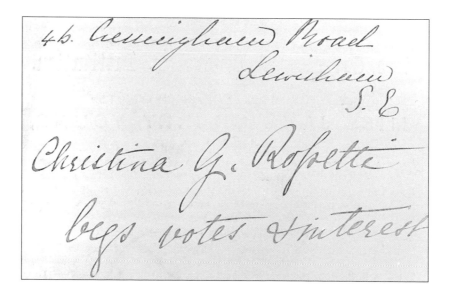

30 Torrington Square
Thursday

Dear Mme Lega Fletcher

Kind you are both in matter and in manner. Your two valued votes <u>are</u> my first actually received.

Pray accept my grateful thanks whilst in hope and fear I remain

Truly Yours
Christina G. Rossetti

*   *   *

30 Torrington Square
W.C.
April 3 1884.

Dear Mme Lega-Fletcher

I have just had the pleasure of placing <u>2</u> on your proxy opposite the last name on the list, Miss Jane C. Young being the lady in whom we are interested. Thank you warmly for so kindly remembering and answering my petition [. . .]

Very truly your obliged
Christina G. Rossetti

*   *   *

30 Torrington Square
W.C.
May 26.

Dear Mme Lega-Fletcher

The candidate you so kindly voted for at the 'Governesses' election just over, failed. But as, standing then for the first time, she polled over 500 votes, it seems hopeful that she may succeed in November if you and others once more lend a helping hand. I therefore venture to remind you of Miss Jane Cherry Young, and to solicit once more your votes and interest for her deserving case.

Very truly yours
Christina G. Rossetti

November 17 1884

Dear Madam Lega-Fletcher

Alas!

Will your kindness hold out and vote next May for Miss Jane Cherry Young? She has missed her election this 3rd time; but having accumulated 902 votes in all, looks forward with some hope to the next governess poll. And even if you cannot favour us yet again, she and I remain gratefully your debtors

Very truly yours
Christina G. Rossetti

*   *   *

1884
5 Station Road
Birchington-on-Sea
October 9.

Dear Mme Lega-Fletcher

Thank you for the substantial kindness of your Votes, and for the special personal kindness of your manner. I am hoping and fearing for poor Miss Young at the impending Poll.

Very gratefully yours
Christina G Rossetti.

*   *   *

Oct 1885
30 Torrington Square – W.C.
Wednesday.

My dear Mme Lega Fletcher

I may well feel abashed at hearing from you this morning and at receiving your Proxy, when last May the candidate you have so kindly and perseveringly assisted was so fortunate as to be elected. I soon afterwards was entrusted with her thanks for all her patronesses within my circle – will you, even thus late, receive them gratefully from her and from myself? – Gratefully, I of course mean, on <u>our</u> parts.

To soothe myself I venture to send you by parcel post my last little book 'Time Flies', and I trust you will not reject a copy in which I have written your name.

> Always your obliged friend
> Christina G. Rossetti.
> I return the precious proxy.

Christina G. Rossetti, Autograph Letters to Mme Lega-Fletcher, Brotherton Collection, (December 1883–October 1885).

SICK WITH STANDING

The lengthy and tortuous process of obtaining an annuity reminds us that many governesses ultimately failed in their bid. For these women, there were few options indeed; many faced destitution, unless, as in Charlotte Yonge's Hopes and Fears, *they were fortunate enough to be adopted by some charitable private individual.*

Seven years more, and Honora was in mourning for her mother. She was alone in the world, without any near or precious claim, those clinging tendrils of her heart rent from their oldest, surest earthly stay, and her time left vacant from her dearest, most constant occupation. Her impulse was to devote herself and her fortune at once to the good work which most engaged her imagination, but Humfrey Charlecote, her sole relation, since heart complaint had carried off his sister Sarah, interfered with the authority he had always exercised over her, and insisted on her waiting one full year before pledging herself to anything. At one-and-thirty, with her golden hair and light figure, her delicate skin and elastic step, she was still too young to keep house in solitude, and she invited to her home a friendless old governess of her own, sick at heart with standing for the Governess's Institution, promising her a daughter's care and attendance on her old age.

Charlotte M. Yonge, *Hopes and Fears* (1899), p. 17.

A PROMISING PROSPECTUS

As early as 1845, there were calls for the GBI to address some of the more fundamental problems of the governessing life. The lack of formal training for governesses has already been alluded to several times. This early report in The Times *suggests that plans for Queen's College (finally opened in 1848) had been in the pipeline for some time.*

GOVERNESSES. – A society is about to be established for the purpose of raising the condition of the very useful class of persons called governesses, and of improving the means of preparatory education which is to enable them to undertake the instruction of others. The prospectus, which is dictated in a truly benevolent spirit, remarks, 'In order to form governesses who may hope eventually to be regarded as the friends of the parents, after establishing a claim to their gratitude, we must select minds whose natural endowments will enable them to profit by the advantages bestowed, and ascertain that they have also a turn for imparting instruction. Accomplishments must hold a due place, and remarkable talents in any line will not be neglected. Cheerfulness and energy will be promoted and encouraged, and these may be aided by the cultivation of kindly affections, the encouragement of innocent amusements, and the formation of habits of self-control. Three months' gratuitous instruction will be offered to pupils properly recommended, and willing to go through the required probationary residence. If admitted, 50*l*. annually paid by them will include the best masters, and every other expense, during three or four years of training.' Among the ladies of rank and station at the head of this society we perceive the names of the Countesses of Mount Edgecombe and Rosebery, Dowager Lady Lyttclton, Lady Noel Byron, and the Hon. Miss Murray.

'Governesses,' *The Times* (25 March, 1845),
p. 5.

The Sweetest Wine Makes the Best Vinegar

*The very idea of ladies obtaining a training for work was repugnant
and incongruous to some. Moreover, many thought a college
education, revolving largely around academic subjects, was
somewhat superfluous to requirements. Even Charlotte Brontë,
otherwise a stalwart supporter of any effort to improve the
governess's portion, questioned the utility of such training,
suggesting that those qualities truly necessary in a governess were
unteachable. In a letter to the publisher W.S. Williams in 1848, she
wrote, 'The Governesses' Institution may be an excellent thing in
some points of view – but it is both absurd and cruel to attempt to
raise still higher the standard of acquirements. Already Governesses
are not half nor a quarter paid for what they teach – nor in most
instances is half or a quarter of their attainments required by their
pupils. The young teacher's chief anxiety, when she sets out in life,
always is, to know a great deal; her chief fear that she should not
know enough; brief experience will, in most instances, shew her that
this anxiety has been misdirected. She will rarely be found too
ignorant for her pupils. The demands on her knowledge will not
often be larger than she can answer; but on her patience, on her self-
control the requirement will be enormous; on her animal spirits (and
woe be to her if these fail!) the pressure will be immense.' (Charlotte
Brontë to W.S. Williams, 12 May 1848)*
In the same vein, Punch, *as ever keenly attuned to the problems of
the governess life, wittily envisaged a college in which governesses
were not only taught an enormous range of academic subjects – an
apparently ridiculous proposition in itself – but also received
instruction in the more intangible requisites of governess life.*

College for Governesses

It is proposed, as we learn from the newspapers, to found an
establishment of this kind, in connection with the Governesses'
Benevolent Institution. We have, however, seen no prospectus of the
course of instruction to be followed, the examinations to be undergone,

or the degrees to be conferred. Any school for the Education of Governesses ought to have a special regard to the duties this class of females has to discharge, and the discipline of mind required by their position. Keeping this in view, we beg to furnish the following hints to the founders of this useful place of instruction: –

In the first place, the pupils admitted must be ladies, both in habits, appearance, manners, and, if possible, birth. This is indispensable. Those who are to have the training of young ladies must belong to the order themselves. They must be sweet-tempered. This is necessary, as their dispositions are likely to have a good deal of souring; and we all know the sweetest wine makes the best vinegar. Their constitutions ought to be strong. It is probable they will lead a close and sedentary life, and the wear and tear of the school-room is no joke. Above all, they must be cheerful. Elasticity is highly necessary in everybody required to support heavy weights. They must be humble, as in that case they will be spared many disappointments; and respectful themselves, as they must not consider they have a claim for respect on any person in the establishment they belong to. They must be able to win the affections of the children intrusted to them, but must beware of indulging affections on their own account.

Thus much for the young persons themselves. Now let us see how their natural qualities are to be most effectually cultivated by the collegiate course of instruction.

Imprimis, this instruction must obviously be universal. A Governess, to judge from the advertisements, is expected to know everything. The course should at least embrace Hebrew (with the points), Greek, Latin, the modern languages of course, the elements of the natural sciences, Zoology, Botany, Mineralogy, Conchology, Geology, Astronomy, with a thorough command of the Globes (to which mothers attach an apparently superstitious importance), Geography, *with maps* (which is a thing constantly asked for, there appearing to be in use a mysterious kind of geography without them) – the accomplishments, of course, including Singing in the Italian manner, and counterpoint, with all varieties of Drawing and Painting, as well as Modelling, if required. Gymnastics would be desirable, and the Indian Exercises. Above all, however, the Multiplication Table must not be overlooked.

This is the intellectual part of the course, and perhaps the least important. The great object should be the moral training of the Governess. For this we would recommend the employment of a carefully selected staff of Professoresses, after this fashion.

Class of Cheerfulness

PROFESSORESS LADY KNAGGS, a person of singularly aggravating disposition, who will daily use every means of trying the temper of the young persons, until their spirits are thoroughly broken, and subject them to every variety of petty annoyances. The least appearance of depression to be punished by low diet and extra ill-temper from a sub-tutoress, chosen from the most cantankerous old maids that may be known to the College authorities. The young persons, while in this class, should have each of them half-a-dozen very boisterous children to take charge of for eight hours every day.

Class of Humility

PROFESSORESS THE HON. MRS HARDLINES, a lady of sixteen quarterings, who will for an hour per diem talk at the Governess Class, alluding to any accident of humble birth or reduced fortunes that can be taken hold of, always speaking of each of them as 'that young person,' and snubbing them on the slightest provocation. The HON. MRS HARDLINES should have at her command a regular staff of servants, including a very pert lady's maid, who will at intervals pass down the class, turning up her nose at the young persons, and saying the most offensive things in a half-whisper, with a running accompaniment of 'Well, I'm sures,' and 'Set 'em ups,' and 'Mean creatures,' and similar humiliating phrases, at which every young lady expressing the least annoyance will be turned down for a week, and put under the discipline of the lower servants, who will repeat similar things in coarser ways.

While in this class the young persons will be lodged in small rooms, and dine exclusively on luke-warm legs of mutton, and the smallest beer.

Class of Self-respect

In this class the discipline of the Humility Class may be carried farther. Instead of the servants, a staff of fashionable young men should be employed to make dishonourable proposals, and offer insulting attentions to the young persons, who will thus be practised in the art of respecting themselves under difficulties, which they will often have to put in practice in their situations.

By pursuing a course of training similar to that sketched above, we may hope to satisfy employers, while we remove the many querulous representations now made of the hardships of Governesses, by supplying a corps of young people thoroughly broken in to the worst they can possibly expect to encounter in after-life.

'College for Governesses', *Punch* (2 October 1847), p. 131.
(Order amended by the editors.)

Fig. 33 A governess undergoes training in humility. (*Punch*, 1847)

TRAINING FOR GOVERNESSES OR EDUCATION FOR FEMALES?

Joking aside, the real Queen's College opened in Harley Street in 1848 (taking the premises next door to the Home for Disengaged Governesses) and was an immediate success.

Mary Maurice's brother Frederick, one of the founders of Queen's College, was one of the ablest defenders of its role in a world of changing economic and social circumstances. Intending initially to reinforce the credentials and training of governesses, the scheme's initiators soon persuaded themselves that only a much broader curriculum and catchment would answer all the contingencies of governess life. Hence the paradox that a scheme aimed at consolidating the system of private, domestic education actually accelerated the growth of public provision for middle-class girls. The passage below reminds us of the mounting pressure upon the middle classes to provide a structured educational system for their children, given the increasingly organized nature of working-class education.

It is proposed immediately after Easter to open a College in London for the Education of Females. The word 'College,' in this connexion, has to English ears a novel and an ambitious sound. I wish we could have found a simpler which would have described our object as well. Since we have chosen this, we should take pains to explain the sense in which we use it; to shew, if we can shew truly, that we are not devising a scheme to realise some favourite theory, but are seeking, by humble and practical methods, to supply an acknowledged deficiency. For this purpose, and not that I may prove the superiority of our plan to all others, I have been requested to address you now.

[. . .]

The vocation of Teacher is an awful one; you cannot do her real good, she will do others unspeakable harm, if she is not aware of its awfulness. Merely to supply her with necessaries, merely to assist her in procuring them for herself – though that is far better, for in so doing you awaken energy of character, reflection, providence – is not fitting her for her work; you may confirm her in the notion that the task of training an immortal spirit may be just as lawfully undertaken in a case of emergency as that of selling ribands. How can you give a woman self-respect, how can you win for her the respect of others, in whom such a notion, or any modification of it, exists? Your business is, by all means, to dispossess her of it; to make her feel the greatness of her work, and yet to shew her that it can be honestly performed. A Society for the relief of Governesses was bound to consider whether they could be useful for this end; if not, whether they might set at work any agency which should aim at the accomplishment of it. They might, it was thought, at least offer certificates to competent Governesses. But then they must have some means of testing their competency; there must be an examination. The members of the benevolent society could not, as such, conduct it; they invited Gentlemen who were in the habit of examining and teaching to form a Committee for the purpose. This Committee soon heard from others, and discovered themselves, that to do any real good they must go further; they must fit the Governesses for their examination; they must provide an Education for Female Teachers. The task seemed a serious but not an impossible one. Training Institutions for the Mistresses of poorer schools are becoming general; those who have thought most upon Education have proclaimed – Governments, here and abroad, have proclaimed, – that these schools are of far more worth than all the mechanical systems by which we fancied for so long a time that masses of children might be fashioned into men. There was no reason why the teachers of the rich should be excluded from a similar benefit. Here it seemed to some of us that we might stop. We had found a class distinctly marked out, which needed our help; to prepare them should be our object; the enterprise was surely great enough; why need we take in a wider, an almost unlimited field?

It was answered by persons of maturer judgment and greater experience, that our first assumption was a wrong one; we had *not* a definite class to deal with, but one which was continually varying. Those who had no dream of entering upon such a work this year, might be forced by some reverse of fortune to think of it next year; was it well to insist that they should have already committed themselves to duties for which we told them they needed preparation; might not it be an unspeakable relief to their consciences to feel that they had received the preparation? We were asked how we dared to deny that every lady is and must be a teacher – of some person or other, of children, sisters, the poor. Again it was urged that though the mere art of teaching is no doubt worthy of diligent study, and should form a part in all sound education, still the main qualification of a Governess is not an acquaintance with this method or that, but a real grounded knowledge of that which is to be taught, and a sympathy with those who are to learn from her. Shall we not, it was said, be likely to make this knowledge less sound and real, this sympathy less living, if we leave the impression upon our teacher's mind that we are chiefly concerned to put her in possession of a craft which she is to cultivate as if she were the member of a certain guild, and not as if she had interests in common with the rest of her sex? To these arguments I confess that I cannot myself see any satisfactory answer. If we yielded to them, it followed, of course, that we must give our Institution a very general character indeed; it could not be described in any terms but those I have used – one for Female Education.

Frederick Denison Maurice, 'Queen's College, London: Its Objects and Method' (1849), pp. 1–5.

QUEEN'S COLLEGE

A year after the opening of the college, Mary Maurice enthusiastically described the advantages of this public method of training, commenting specifically on the varied backgrounds of the students and the merits of a wide-ranging and well-organized curriculum. Students at Queen's were chaperoned to lectures given by male academics seconded from the nearby King's College. For Mary Maurice this opportunity to enjoy the teaching of 'superior men' was the most striking asset of the course.

. . . [T]he still more important work, that of providing the very best education for Teachers, is in full operation, and is already realizing the sanguine expectations of its founders, and encouraging the earnest zeal of those professors who have heartily aided in the scheme.

[. . .]

Classes are formed on all subjects, to which ladies above the age of twelve are admitted. After mature deliberation, it was determined that a greater advantage would be secured by placing side by side different ranks of society, than by restricting the College to one only. The exclusive feeling which the teaching of a peculiar class would create was thus prevented, and it was thought that the future governess would be raised in the estimation of her employers, if distinguished amongst them by successful industry. Many of her fellow-students might be connected with families to which hereafter she might be introduced, and they would early learn to respect and esteem their companion in study. [. . .] Many have complained of the injury which would accrue to private establishments in consequence of the superior advantages offered on reasonable terms in this public institution; but private good must always be sacrificed to public advantage – as railroads were not prevented because the reduced number of travellers would injure the turnpike roads; so the rapid movements of education cannot be kept back for a similar reason. Combination is necessary to accomplish a great end, and without the admission of a large number of pupils, the services of the first-rate professors could not be obtained. Schools are, however, allowed to share the same privileges, and some are gladly availing themselves of the permission.

Separate classes are formed for theology, moral, mental, and natural philosophy, modern and ancient history, English literature, composition, and grammar, reading, geography, arithmetic, and the mathematics. Also for the Latin, German, French, and Italian languages, for drawing and painting, either in figure or landscape, for music, both vocal, instrumental, and scientific, and for instruction in the art of teaching.

To these are added gratuitous Evening Classes, on the same subjects, for Governesses who are employed during the day, and classes are now commenced for younger pupils, to prepare them for deriving the full benefit of afterwards being admitted to the College.

Courses of Lectures are also given on different branches of science. Each pupil is allowed to select the studies to which she desires to attend, and to join only in such as she thinks desirable.

The rapid increase of the students proves that the public is beginning duly to estimate the advantages thus provided for female education.

Every arrangement is made to promote the comfort and accommodation of the pupils, who, though not resident, may remain at the College during the class hours, and pursue their studies in the intervals between the lessons.

A Library for reference is in the course of formation, and maps and other facilities for improvement are provided.

Ladies are appointed as visitors, who are present in rotation, to see that the regulations of the College are duly observed. The studies are so varied as to produce the strongest motive to exertion, without the false stimulus of emulation.

Those who have hitherto learned on the ordinary method, can here share benefits which can be met with only in a public institution, where the Professors consecrate their talents to the noble object of training the future instructors of the rising generation. However excellent the teaching of some women may be for young children, it must be admitted, that after the elements of education have been imparted, the highest advantage is derived from the teaching of superior men. Their greater depth of thought and reflection, and the mental discipline to which they have been subjected, enable them most effectually to inform and enlarge the minds of others. Their acquaintance with the laws of language, and the sources whence it is derived, lead them to regard with solemnity the words they employ, and thus give a depth of meaning to phrases and forms of speech of which those not so initiated have no conception. The tendency of women's minds to use desultory and unmeaning phraseology is corrected when they have the benefit of such instruction, and they unconsciously receive a stimulus to exertion. They see that education is not learning by heart, that task-work is not development of mind, and that the knowledge of books is not wisdom. They perceive that if ever they are to exercise a useful influence over others it must be by awakening their faculties, by calling out their energies, by showing them that the cultivation of the mind is the highest prerogative, and will bring rich fruits to reward the toil.

Another advantage to be derived from this source is, that of effectually destroying all conceit of their own superiority. Pigmies who lived in the society of giants would not boast of their height.

[Mary Maurice], *Governesses Life: Its Trials, Duties and Encouragements* (1849), pp. 1–5.

A DRASTIC SOLUTION

The assorted activities of the GBI met with considerable success. By the 1860s sister societies had opened in Liverpool, Manchester, and Edinburgh and in 1869 the Northern Counties Society for Granting Annuities to Governesses and other Ladies was established. Nevertheless, the number of governesses who actually benefited from the services of these societies could be but small. With increasing numbers of middle-class women desperately seeking governessing work throughout the 1850s, other solutions had to be found. Emigration to the expanding colonies, particularly Australia, New Zealand and South Africa seemed, to many, a favourable alternative to impoverishment in the less comfortable climes of Britain. Through the tireless endeavours of Maria Rye, a member of the Society for Promoting the Employment of Women, the hitherto rather piecemeal efforts to send women to the colonies using funds donated by individuals were formalized in 1862. The Female Middle Class Emigration Society was formed. The rules of the society, with their demand for domestic as well as academic talents, their strict concern for the repayment of loans, and their vague promise of a 'situation', illustrate how uncertain must have been the expectations of these cultivated émigrées. How they fared in their adopted lands is a question beyond the scope of this book, but one ably addressed by Patricia Clarke in The Governesses: Letters from the Colonies 1862–1882 *(1985).*

Rules of the FMGES

1. The society confines its assistance entirely to educated women – no applicants being accepted who are not sufficiently educated to undertake the duties of nursery governess.

2. Every applicant is examined as far as possible, with regard to her knowledge of cooking, baking, washing, needlework and housework, and is required to be willing to assist in these departments of labour should it be necessary.

3. Applicants are required to give the names and addresses of four persons as referees, from whom the society can obtain information respecting the position, character, strength, qualities, and general suitableness of the applicant for a colonial life, two of these referees to be ladies with whom the applicant has held situations, and two to be her personal friends. The references are, if possible, taken up personally by the Secretaries, and the Society hopes, by establishing correspondents in the chief provincial towns, to ensure in all cases a personal interview with the applicant, if not with her referees.

4. If the information obtained is satisfactory, the applicant, being accepted by the Society, receives all possible needful assistance. Should she be unable to pay the entire cost of outfit and passage money, the Society advances the deficient amount, a legal agreement to repay within two years and four months being signed by the emigrant, and two respectable householders as securities. Should an approved applicant not require a loan, she is equally entitled to the advantages of the Society's care and protection.

5. The Society secures all passages and purchases cabin fittings on behalf of the emigrants, thus saving much trouble and time. It is also enabled by the liberality of shipowners and outfitters to effect a considerable saving of expense. The Society's assistance to emigrants is given free of any charge whatever.

6. The Society has established regular correspondents at most of the colonial ports. As soon as a party leaves England, notice of their departure is sent by the Overland Mail to the correspondent at the port to which the emigrants are bound, a list of their names and qualifications, together with copies of the testimonials of each applicant, are sent at the same time and as the notice is received six weeks before the emigrants arrive, there is time to make preparations for their reception, and even to seek for situations.

Patricia Clarke, *The Governesses: Letters from the Colonies* (1985), pp. 11–12.

A LION HEART AND A MARTYR SPIRIT

To some extent, benevolent activities on behalf of the governess helped to foster the public image of her defencelessness and vulnerability; as we have already noted, however, the underlying aim of much charitable work was actually to promote self-reliance among governesses. It seems likely, for example, that the improved education and training offered to governesses from the mid-century onwards cultivated a sense of self-worth among the new generation. Though reformers could not correct the abuses suffered by the governess within individual family homes, their efforts may well have encouraged individual acts of assertiveness and pluck. In Harriet Smythies' aptly titled novel, The Daily Governess: or, Self-Dependence *(1861), Lucy Blair, employed for just two weeks by the Treherne family, arrives at her appointment soaked to the skin after a violent rainstorm, and is reprimanded by her employer for infecting the children with a cold. Her exhilarating response affords a timely blow at the traditional representation of the poor, unprotected governess.*

Lucy was roused. 'What you call the Treherne cold, madam,' she replied, 'is very like influenza; and if your daughters are certain to have caught it from my damp clothes, which surely would be more likely to affect me, I had better discontinue my visits. It is difficult enough as it is to arouse their attention, and conquer confirmed habits of sloth; but if perfect prostration ensues, I can be of no use here.'

Lady Hamilton Treherne was perfectly astounded at the calm self-assertion and dignified independence of this speech. She gazed at Lucy with a cold, insolent stare, which, however, gradually changed, as she met the proud, mournful, and somewhat reproachful gaze of Lucy's beautiful eyes. Amazement kept her ladyship silent. Hannah and Annette looked on, almost with the interest people do at a race or fight. There lay, lapped in luxury, canopied with crimson velvet, couched on down, robed in cambric, lace, and cashmere, waited on by obsequious flatterers, and fed with dainties from Sèvres china and silver plate, the still handsome, selfish, aristocratic employer; and there stood – her damp, old, black silk dress clinging to her slight Psyche form, her wet hair gathered and knotted up at the back of her head, ill-clad, poorly-fed, overworked, but with a lion heart, a martyr spirit, and the flush of modest worth stung to resentment by heartless insolence – the Daily Governess! And the native dignity of the girl triumphed over the cruel insolence and acquired coolness of the woman; and Lady Hamilton Treherne dropped her eyes, and raising them with a softened coaxing expression said –

'If I did not allude to the danger of your taking cold yourself, Miss Blair, it was because, from your perfect indifference to the state of your clothes, I thought you might be used, as many very respectable people are, to be out in all weathers.'

'So far from it, madam,' said Lucy, 'the life I led, till I accepted your situation, was one of so much seclusion and shelter that I scarcely remember ever having been caught in a shower in my life.'

'Dear me!' exclaimed Lady Hamilton Treherne; 'I had no idea of this – I wish I had known it. I thought daily governesses were almost (from constant exposure to the elements) as weatherproof as sailors.'

'I made my *début* as a daily governess in this house a fortnight ago, madam; and if, as you anticipate, the young ladies will not be able to their studies at present, I am quite ready to resign the office. I have many more applications, and – forgive me for saying so – some which promise more docility in the pupils and more sympathy in the parents.'

As Lucy spoke, the tears sparkled in her eyes, and her cheek paled and glowed alternately. Hannah, at the other end of the room, whispered to Annette, 'There's a spirit, and she's only a daily!' And Annette, with a Frenchwoman's ready pity for the oppressed, exclaimed, 'Poor tin'! *la pauvrette!* she won't get no sympatee here from my lady, and no doceelity from her pupils, I don't tink!'

Lady Hamilton Treherne, who before this interview, had intended to humble, but not to dismiss Lucy (whose talents were of so rare an order, and who took such conscientious pains with her pupils), valued her all the more highly, as she saw how ready she was to resign her thankless and laborious task.

Mrs Harriet Gordon Smythies, *The Daily Governess; or,*
Self-Dependence, (1861), pp. 28–31.

CHAPTER 5

MADEMOISELLE, FRÄULEIN OR MISS? THE GOVERNESS AND NATIONAL IDENTITIES

Surviving memoirs of genteel Victorian girlhood feature a disproportionate number of French and German, rather than British governesses, perhaps because memoirs tend to be written by and about the élite – the especially rich, successful or famous – rather than the ordinary. However the French Revolution and its aftermath, and the uprisings of 1848, did see significant numbers of Prussian, French and Swiss women seeking refuge and employment in Britain. Kathryn Hughes (1993, p. 105) observes that the National Census of 1861 found 1,408 foreign governesses resident in Britain, capitalizing, it would seem, on the importance of modern languages to an elegant feminine education. Pamela Horn (1989, p. 339) notes that the Post Office Directory for London in 1880 listed three organizations dealing specifically with Swiss and German governesses. Many of these women were better educated than their British counterparts though some came from homes quite as penurious as that of the 'seen better days' British spinster pitied by philanthropists in Chapter 4, and often suffered the added burdens of enforced migration, culture shock and exile. As historians have noted (Peterson, 1972), the very fact of their foreign provenance could sanction the relaxing, or at least blurring, of the rigid class and gender distinctions that made for the 'Governess Problem'. The awkwardness inherent in the governess's role, and the embarrassments to which her position, history and conduct might give rise, could in such cases be attributed to national differences and passed over with a condescending smile.

For many middle-class commentators, however, more was at stake than assuaging embarrassment. *Mademoiselle* might offer elegance and an exquisite Parisian accent to the aristocratic schoolroom, but these advantages might be more than outweighed by what was seen as her dubious moral influence as a Catholic and as a Frenchwoman. Francophobia and anti-Catholicism had, since the late-eighteenth century, combined to cast serious doubt on the religious, ethical and sexual probity of the French governess in many fictional and advice works. In the nineteenth century, the spiritual and theological superiority of evangelical protestantism was for many a badge of national honour, not to be ceded even to the 'outward conformity' of a German or a Swiss. Those who could afford to do so often hired a French *bonne* (think of Adela's nurse in *Jane Eyre*) or bought in conversation lessons in German, French or Italian, while maintaining a strong native presence in the schoolroom itself.

If hiring a foreign governess suggested itself to some families as a way of cutting the gordian knot of her 'status incongruence', travelling abroad must have promised similar advantages for the British governess herself. We have seen in Chapter 4 that the prospect of subsidized and more or less organized emigration was offered to, and indeed accepted by, some Victorian governesses as a solution to their personal poverty and to their apparent superfluousness to the population at large. In this chapter, however, we are concerned with the ideological and cultural implications of the decision to work overseas. Throughout the century Britain's imperial and industrial strength lent considerable international consequence to her culture, institutions and manners, as well as to the English language itself. Hence the prestige enjoyed by continental instructresses in aristocratic British homes was mirrored by the high reputation of the English 'Miss' among the merchant and professional classes, not to mention noble and even royal families, in many parts of the world.

The fact that such women helped to consolidate a sense of national self-confidence at home, while asserting it abroad, is attested by the existence of a significant body of writing dedicated to adventures of the 'English Governess in' a variety of 'exotic' contexts. Such accounts, many of them fictional or fictionalized, have much in common with the popular genres of travel writing and missionary narrative. They presuppose the superiority of British standards of morality, rationality and virtue, and typically use the pretext of an 'insider's view' to comment, more often than not critically, upon the lifestyles of the host nations. Amongst the detailed discussions of festivals and myths, political intrigues, diet and costume, kin structures, living arrangements and child rearing priorities, all presented in a way calculated to appeal to British complacency, it is difficult to gauge how these migrant teachers actually fared, and whether they were in fact exempted from the sufferings of their counterparts at home. In selecting from this often violently partisan, and sometimes xenophobic literature, we have attempted to highlight ways in which the governess's alien status might inflect or inform how she represented, to herself and others, the day-to-day challenges of her working life.

An Eccentric Exile in 1820s London

In the wake of the French Revolution, communities of high-born French exiles sprang up in London and elsewhere. Among the British aristocracy patronage of such individuals, often as masters or governesses to their own children, signalled international solidarity and noblesse oblige, *while shoring up the family's cosmopolitan image. Differences of language, manners and beliefs that in other contexts might have been regarded with suspicion, were here construed as part of* mademoiselle's *charm.*

When I was quite small, we removed to 8 Upper Grosvenor Street, a house associated with the memory of my first governess, Mlle. Clémence Isaure Angélique, daughter of the Vicomte d'Albenas, a French nobleman who had emigrated to England during the Revolution, and who, like so many other members of the aristocracy, had encountered the slings and arrows of outrageous Fortune so keenly that Mlle. Clémence was obliged to earn her living as a governess, instead of enjoying the life her birth and attractions merited. I remember her as a handsome girl of nineteen, charming, but a little *difficile*, for she had fads which were not understood or tolerated in those days when girls were more 'sensible' than they are now.

Mlle. Clémence disliked meat, and would never eat it, a whim which was considered very 'odd,' and she also refused to wear any flannel garments. The result of this was that poor Mlle. Clémence went into a decline which caused her death, at least we were always told so, perhaps with the idea of pointing a moral to young people who hated flannel.

Countess of Cardigan and Lancastre, *My Recollections* (1909), pp. 3–4.

A WEALTHY SCOTS SCHOOLROOM OF THE MID-CENTURY

As the century progressed, Prussian and Swiss governesses competed with Frenchwomen for the most prestigious posts in Britain. The high reputation of German scholarship, education and teacher training, and the presence of German governesses at Windsor Castle combined to give the edge to the Fräulein *as the instructress of choice in many prosperous homes. Despite frequent removals from one prestigious rented residence to another in Scotland in the 1850s, Lucy Walford's father ensured continuity in the education of his five daughters by hiring not one, but two German governesses. Once established there, the pair imbued the schoolroom, and indeed the household as a whole, with distinctively German tastes and habits.*

Governesses were naturally important personages with us in the Blackhall days. We were five sisters, and my parents were great educationalists: accordingly one preceptress was not considered sufficient, and we had two – both Germans, and related to each other.

The German craze in the educational world was at its height, taking its cue no doubt from the Royal schoolroom, then in full swing; furthermore, I believe that my mother, when debating the question of having a Parisian for our No 2 was daunted by the fear of internecine warfare, or at any rate of jealousy between Fräulein and Mademoiselle. Accordingly there they were. Fräulein Lindemann, fair, soft, pretty, with heavenly blue eyes, and a pure soprano voice; and Fräulein Muller, ugly, dark, eager, strenuous, with spectacles, and a fierce contralto.

Both were singers, and musical evenings soon became *de rigueur* in the house. The two voices not only blended charmingly, but had been trained to sing together. An invitation having been sent in due time to the schoolroom, the pair would enter arm-in-arm, carefully and becomingly dressed, with rolls of music in their hands. By-and-by, when the sweet songs of the Vaterland thrilled a delighted audience, some of the latter would be proud to join in; the group round the piano would swell, and my mother – an excellent musician – would readily act as accompanist, adding her own sweet low tones from time to time, timidly, but with keen enjoyment.

It needed but a very little pressure on the part of the younger ones to gain her permission to sit up an extra half-hour on these occasions; hence I remember them now. Let it be remembered how early were the hours we kept.

At other times the Fräuleins spent their evenings together in the schoolroom, happily enough, no doubt, reading, working, and writing letters. It would have been a tax on them to have had to dress and go into company every night, and it was not as though one poor exiled girl had been left to solitude and her own devices. They were both clever, efficient, and thoroughly trained, with diplomas from various colleges. They taught us well; and we acquired from them many things besides the knowledge they were engaged to impart.

Our schoolroom was a kingdom in itself, and there we might do as we chose, and as the Fräuleins chose. If, under their auspices, we elected to cook nice little puddings and pastries such as were compounded in their native land, no one had anything to say. We sent to the kitchen for what we wanted; we brought in fruit from the garden, berries from the hillsides; and the kind creatures, especially if we had been diligent at our lessons, would hasten to bring out the little stewpans. Then what a delicious odour arose, and how ravishing tasted the small, steaming mess cooked by our own hands! I doubt that any English preceptress, either of that date or any other date, would have so condescended with her pupils.

[. . .]

What the governess thought of our Scottish Sunday as represented at Blackhall, can only be surmised, for they were at once too cautious and too loyal ever to let it out.

They were completely happy with us – that I know. Their warmly affectionate natures made them soon look on our house as a home, and they learned to climb the hills and rove over the surrounding country as to the manner born.

> Lucy Bethia Walford, *Recollections of a Scottish Novelist*
> (1984, written 1910), pp. 31–3.

REMEMBERED CRUELTIES

Such glowing reminiscences as Lucy Walford's must, of course, be handled with care, taking into account the effects both of nostalgia and of Walford's subsequent career as a writer of fiction. The following, rather later, memoir of a childhood in the 1870s is considerably less fond. Lady Angela Forbes served her country as a volunteer in France during the First World War, working in a hospital and later organizing canteens for the British soldiers. Her account bears the stamp of twentieth-century anti-German feeling as well as of memory's tendency to caricature.

General knowledge and common-sense were early inculcated, and special intelligence received its just reward, my brother Harry being tipped for looking out cross-country journeys in the Bradshaw correctly! But there was another side to the medal, and I remember once having my ears boxed at luncheon for not knowing the Latin name for maidenhair fern!

I used to be delighted when our governesses came under the fire of father's questions; though they didn't admit it, they dreaded the ordeal, and I was not in the least sorry for them.

Those dreadful German governesses! How I grew to hate them and their horrid language! How many miserable hours, as I grew older, I spent over those Goethe and Schiller recitations.

French came quite naturally to me. I really think I spoke it before I spoke English. I had an old French nurse whom I adored, and I can well remember now the dreadful agony I went through saying good-bye to her when she left me to go to the Gerards. I saw her a few days afterwards in the Park, and I cried so loudly that she had to bring me home herself; the people who heard me and who didn't know the facts must have thought me a much-injured or very naughty child.

I detested the governess who presided over our destinies at this time, and I didn't like her any better for her treatment of me after this episode, for she inveigled me into her room with the promise of chocolates, and when she got me safely there, gave me a sound smacking. I think this legend shows that even the most careful parents dwell often in a state of blissful ignorance of how their precious offspring are faring upstairs.

Angela Forbes, *Memories and Base Details* (1921), pp. 14–15.

ENGLISHNESS PREFERRED

Though the hiring of French and German governesses clearly went into and out of vogue, there was more involved than mere fashion, or the acquisition of a pure accent. To some extent the supposed relative merits of French, English and German governesses were simply part of the currency of genteel conversation. More importantly, for their employers they represented competing ways of asserting national identity: through the expression of religious integrity, linguistic competency or cultural tradition. A decision to have one's children educated this way or that could also reinforce a particular version of British domesticity and family. Charlotte Yonge's advice book Womankind *comes out firmly in favour of the home-grown governess, middle-class angst notwithstanding.*

For my own part I much prefer English to foreign governesses. The absence of unity in doctrine seems to me a heavy price to pay for slightly better pronunciation of the language, &c. What after all is the outward conformity of the Swiss or German Protestant? Who knows

OPPORTUNISM.

Mrs. Verdant Green (who is parting with her German Governess). "OH, BUT, FRÄULEIN, YOU WOULD NEVER DO FOR THE ST. ALBYNS; THEY'RE ROMAN CATHOLICS, YOU KNOW; AND YOU GAVE ME TO UNDERSTAND, WHEN YOU CAME TO US, THAT YOU WERE OF AN OLD LUTHERAN FAMILY."
Proud Daughter of an Ancient Race. "ACH, VORKIF ME, MATAM, FOR LETTING YOU SINK I VAS A BRODESTANT! I VAS REALLY A ROMAN GASSOLIC ALL ZE TIME; LIKE MY NOPLE ANCESTORS IN ZE MITTLE AITCHFS, ZE COUNTS VON MEYER-OPPENHFIM ZU HIRSCH-GOLDSMID-ROSENBERG, WHO FOUGHT IN ZE GRUSATES!"

Fig. 34 'Opportunism!' (*Punch*, 1896)

under what circumstances the children may be left to the governess's guidance, and is it not best that she should be really of their Church? Besides, if history is not to be learnt by rote, but thoughtfully, should it not be read with one whose principles and opinions are the same with ours? And another point is worthy of consideration. It is not right to condemn a whole nation, but it is notorious that the French standard of truth, is very unlike the English, especially in Roman Catholics. Of course there are many excellent foreign governesses, but on the whole, it seems to me that the character has much greater chance of being formed by a fellow-countrywoman and Churchwoman.

[...]

People generally say that grammar is better learnt through another language than our own; and this is true to a certain extent, provided they do not mean colloquial French through a *bonne*, and German by the Ollendorf method. I say only to a certain extent, even when the second language has been really and grammatically learnt, because, though a general knowledge of grammar in the abstract is thus acquired, the idioms and peculiarities of the acquired tongue are the study, while our own are left to the light of nature, practice, and observation. It seems to me that after the first baby foundations of the parts of speech are laid, and ordinary speech and writing made correct, that one foreign grammar, no matter what, should be thoroughly taught, and then that the construction of any additional language will be easily acquired, while in the latter year or two of education, some very thorough book on English grammar should be well got up. Those provided for training-schools are generally excellent of their kind; and the practice of thorough analyzing [sic] a sentence is a very useful one. It is a good thing when grammar passes into logic; and though even the rudiments of logic are a little beyond the schoolroom grasp of mind, a girl who has the capacity would do well to cultivate them, not so much for their own sake, as because the power of reasoning is a most important element in having a right judgment in all things.

As to other languages, French is a necessity. To speak it with perfect ease and a Parisian accent is a useful and graceful accomplishment, only to be acquired by intercourse with natives early enough in life for the organs to be flexible; but this is only exceptionally an entire matter of necessity. French after 'the school of Stratford-le-Bowe' has been prevalent among educated Englishwomen ever since Chaucer's time; and a thorough grammatical knowledge, with such pronunciation as can be obtained through good lessons, is to stay-at-home people more valuable than mere ease of speech, which they only rarely have to exercise.

But if it be needful, a German *bonne* is generally kind, true, and faithful, and not likely to do harm to little children. It is the further advantage in making this pronunciation a nursery, not a schoolroom matter, that no girl reading ancient history with a foreigner has a chance of hearing the usual English pronunciation of classical names. To me it seems that the fashion of teaching German as a matter of course is rather a pity. I had rather make Latin the schoolroom lesson, and leave German to be volunteered afterwards. German is so difficult, as to require a great deal of time; and it is so irregular, as not to be the key to nearly so much as Latin – in learning which it is quite possible to learn the great outlines of both French and Italian – at any rate, the study of both, alike in construction and words, is much simplified, since both are Latin broken in different ways. German leads to nothing (except in the case of philology) but reading its own literature; whereas Latin is needful for clear knowledge of our own tongue, and moreover gives much greater facility of comprehension and power of exactness in the terminology of every other science, from Theology downwards.

Charlotte Yonge, *Womankind* (1876), pp. 37–41.

DISPATCHED

A governess's situation symbolized her employers' – and by extension their nation's – reputation as 'civilized' and 'cultured'. It could also be interpreted in a different way, as manifesting the host country's indifference or negligence. The debate about the 'Governess Question' frequently treated the fate of individual governesses as symptomatic of national moral health, as in this description of an English governess's return from France.

The Treatment of Governesses in France and England

[To the Editor of The Times]

Sir,– Public attention having been called to the recent lamentable death of a young French lady in this town, I think it desirable to state that a very similar case occurred here about four months since, but in that case the sufferer was a young Englishwoman, aged 22, who had been in the service of a French lady of rank, residing in the Faubourg St. Germain, at Paris. On the arrival of the evening train from Paris she was found in one of the carriages in a state of delirium, which, on her being removed to an hotel and medical aid called in, was found to arise from malignant typhus. It was only by means of her passport and a few incoherent words that her name and that of her native place were elicited. I attended her until her death, but never could obtain from her a single intelligible reply. She proved to be of a very respectable family, and had with her a considerable sum of money for a person in her condition of life, for the security of which no precautions had been taken. Her brother, a respectable tradesman at H—, in Suffolk, was able to arrive only in time to follow her to the grave. There can be no doubt whatever that she must have been in a terrible condition of fever when she was put into the railway carriage.

I have communicated these facts because there seems, I think, to be a disposition in some quarters to put an unjust construction on the late most deplorable occurrences.

Inhumanity is, unhappily, peculiar to no one country or nation.

I am Sir, your obedient servant,

AN ENGLISH CHAPLAIN

Boulogne-sur-Mer, Dec. 15.

'English Chaplain', 'Treatment of Governesses in France and England', *The Times* (18 December 1857), p. 5.

THE WASTE LANDS OF MIND, OR THE EDEN OF MATRIMONY?

The two-way traffic in governesses, languages, cultures – and reputations – between the schoolrooms of Britain and mainland Europe was to be complicated and extended by the mid-century furore over 'surplus women'. This controversy, as we have seen, led many governesses to emigrate to the colonies. The staff of Punch, *hearty supporters of the governess for the most part, could not resist a joke at the idea of this latest cultural export.*

The Governess Abroad

Out of their own country, prophets, it is well known, only obtain honour. A similar remark, we fear, applies to Governesses; but their case is still harder, inasmuch as unlike some prophets – those, for instance, of the Raphael School or Academy of high Astrological Art, they don't receive in lieu of honour any tangible equivalent. We are not surprised, therefore, to hear of a great Governess Emigration Movement.

Our colonial dependencies have wisely declined to accept our periodical complimentary offering of convicts. While appreciating our Sheffield cutlery, they are not to be dazzled by the sharp blades bearing the recognised certificate, 'Town Made.' We should fancy, nevertheless, that they would joyfully hail an argosy freighted with refined and intelligent spinsters. Now that we are at liberty to export our Looms, Engines, and Presses, there is no reason why the machinery of education should be kept at home under lock and key.

Adelaide and Victoria, however, we are told by some rude observers, do not require accomplished governesses. Those pretty young colonies are perfectly competent to manage the kitchen garden, and can very well dispense with a conservatory for some time to come. We think that this conclusion is not well grounded. Who would not be pained to see Victoria and Adelaide a pair of romps with bright eyes and sun-burnt cheeks, and splendid appetites, but aggravating poor letter H beyond all endurance, and making fearful havoc with their papa's veal, wine, and vinegar? Of course, the mother country don't contemplate sending her wealthy daughters a parcel of blue stockings. They might, however, surely find room for a few 'Ologies' without disturbing their culinary stores. DR BUCKLAND and MRS GLASSE could go together arm-in-arm. To be conversant with languages does not imply inability to pickle tongues. An acquaintance with conchology, one would think, would be a fitting preparation for scolloped oysters, and as for pastry, that need not deteriorate by the fair manipulator's having had an insight into the crust of the earth.

Another and still more unpleasant class of censors insinuate that the intending emigrants carry two faces under one hood. While ostensibly going out to cultivate the waste lands of mind their real destination is the Eden of Matrimony. It is rumoured that their ambition is not so much to enlarge the circle of knowledge, as to form a little circle of their own. That, *in fine*, they are bent on making personal conquests rather than in teaching the nascent idea how to shoot. We don't believe a word of it. But admitting it, for sake of argument, what does this lofty impeachment amount to? Simply that they aim at permanently promoting the greatest happiness of the greatest number. Then it is asserted that the nomadic tribes, who wander about in quest of nuggets, eschew marriage, and are not prepared to execute a settlement. If this really be so, we have nothing further to advance. We would not recommend our gently nurtured countrywomen a wanderer's life in a gypsy's tent, and although in this tight little Island there may be a scanty crop of offers, comparing the Exquisites of the Serpentine with the Rovers of Swan River, it can scarcely be doubted that a beau in the hand is worth two in the bush.

'The Governess Abroad', *Punch* (4 October 1862), p. 139.

NO SINECURE

Though the Emigration Movement heightened public awareness of their travels, English-speaking governesses had been taking advantage of their international cachet *for many years, accompanying their employers on continental travels, or seeking well-paid appointments abroad on their own initiative. Anna Bicknell travelled to Paris in 1852 to take up a post as governess to the daughters of the Compte de Tascher de la Pagerie, Grand Master of the Empress Eugénie's household. Humoured for her English manners and tea-drinking habits (a friend, the Archbishop of Bourges, nicknamed her 'Albion'), Bicknell nevertheless reminds us that, even at its most prestigious, governessing could be hard work.*

The next day was Sunday, with mass in the imperial chapel; but on the Monday I began fully the duties of my position, which I soon found was no sinecure, though made as pleasant as possible by the friendly kindness and courtesy of all around me. But from the moment when I was awakened in the morning till a late hour at night there was not an interval of time to breathe. The two girls being of different ages, the professors, classes, lectures, etc., were also totally different; so my days were spent in rushing out with one, and then rushing back to take

165

the other somewhere else; on foot, in all weathers, which the Duchess considered necessary for the health of my pupils; but, as I had two, the fatigue was doubled. During these lectures, etc., I had to take notes incessantly, and to prepare the work for them. Often I was obliged to dress in ten minutes for a large dinner-party, because some professor had prolonged his lesson to the very last moment. The constant mental strain, added to the physical fatigue, was almost more than I could endure, and my health suffered so severely that I greatly feared the impossibility of continuing such an arduous task. In the evening there were dancing lessons three times a week; one at the English embassy, from which we returned at a late hour, and two others at the Tuileries in the apartments of the Duchesse de Bassano, our next neighbour. On the remaining evenings I frequently accompanied the (Princess) Countess, or the Comtesse Stéphanie, to theatres or operas, which, though very agreeable, added considerably to the overwhelming fatigue of the day. As to my own private correspondence, I was obliged to write necessary letters often very late at night, to the great anger of the Duchess, who rightly declared that I was wearing myself out; but I had no other resource. As time went on, matters happily became more easy, and after the marriage of my eldest pupil with Prince Maximilian von Thurn und Taxis, my task was considerably diminished. The work of the first year, however, was absolutely crushing.

Anna L. Bicknell, *Life in the Tuileries under the Second Empire* (1895), pp. 19–20.

THE GOVERNESS AS MISSIONARY

Narratives, fictional or otherwise, of governesses' travels became a significant sub-genre in their own right, appealing to the Victorian taste for the unfamiliar and 'exotic', and, more often than not, confirming the superiority of all things British. Miss M'Crindell's, The English Governess: A Tale of Real Life *(1844) is set on Gibraltar and offers itself as 'a simple narrative, consisting almost entirely of facts, with very little mixture of fiction' intended to*

portray the 'efficacy of vital *religion' and to awaken the 'attention*
of British Christians to the spiritual destitution, and degraded
condition, of unhappy Spain, and her interesting, though
misguided children' (pp. vii–viii). (Her volume ends with a discreet
advertisement for her own educational establishment.)

To curb the wild eccentricities of Isabella, and guide her perverted
mind into the paths of reason and religion; to check the exuberant
spirits of Cecilia, and teach her to find pleasure in more rational
pursuits; to subdue the haughty self-will of Augusta, and bring it under
the influence of the mild, humble, self-denying spirit of the Gospel; and
to control, regulate, and direct to proper objects, the extreme sensibility
and romantic ardour of Eliza; – these were, indeed, results which she
earnestly longed to accomplish, but to which she felt herself utterly
unequal. She was depressed by the view of her own helplessness, and
would have sunk under the discouragement, had she not recollected the
promise that cheered the great apostle of the Gentiles, under far greater
difficulties; 'My grace is sufficient for thee, for my strength is made
perfect in weakness.' She, therefore, resolved, in the spirit of prayer, to
continue her 'work of faith and labour of love', and, in humble
dependence on divine assistance, to adopt every method that seemed
likely to favour her important object.

[. . .]

Christmas day was, with the Romish inhabitants, a season of mingled
riot and devotion. About eight the preceding evening, the bells rang a
noisy peal, when the multitude flocked to the church, to witness the
beginning of those superstitions which were to last all night. After
bowing to the idols there set up for a blind worship, they retired, to
spend the night in the most senseless riot, and scandalous excesses.
Dancing and revelling were universal in every Spanish residence; but,
not satisfied with these, numbers of drunken and disorderly persons
paraded the streets all night, causing so much noise and confusion, that
the peaceable inhabitants found it almost impossible to sleep, and were
continually reminded of the heathen practices prevalent among the

KENT HOUSE

ESTABLISHMENT FOR YOUNG LADIES,

MAISMORE SQUARE, NEW PECKHAM,

CONDUCTED BY

MISSES SANDERS AND M'CRINDELL.

Terms.

Board and instruction in all the essential branches of a French and English education, Writing, Arithmetic, and the Use of the Globes:

TWENTY-FIVE GUINEAS PER ANNUM.

Pupils under ten years of age:

TWENTY-TWO GUINEAS PER ANNUM.

Accomplishments on the usual terms.

Satisfactory references can be given, to the parents of pupils who have been educated in the Establishment.

Misses Sanders and M'Crindell, having been educated in France, can ensure to their pupils advantages which are often unattainable in England; French being not only the language of the schoolroom, but the constant medium of communication at all times, soon becomes so familiar to them, that they acquire, without difficulty, that fluency in the use of it, and that purity of accent, which are indispensable to a polite education. It is the chief aim of the principals, tó form the characters, as well as instruct the minds, of their pupils, through the divine blessing, on a system based on scriptural principles, and conducted with Christian faithfulness and affection.

Fig. 35 'A Polite Education Offered'.

Hindoos, and the poor pagans of central Africa. In the midst of these disgraceful orgies, the rioters visited the church, after midnight, to rock the cradle of the waxen Jesus, which was then exhibited, and to pay their adorations to the senseless idol, and the other dolls, representing Mary and Joseph!

R. M'Crindell, *The English Governess* (1844), pp. 90, 173–4.

BETWEEN EMPIRES

Armed with their copies of Mangnall's Questions *and a set of globes, some ventured even further afield. Throughout the century Moscow was favoured as a glamorous destination by many English governesses – some of whom ultimately found themselves caught up in the Revolution of 1917. Purportedly the story of a real governess of the author's acquaintance, E.H. Hamilton's* The English Governess in Russia *(1861), like M'Crindell's story above,*

is a narrative with a purpose: 'to give information to a large class
of English ladies who seek employment in Russia, in the capacity
of governesses' and 'to benefit Russia herself . . . in a matter of
vital moment, – we mean the education of her children' (p. iii).
This deceptively simple narrative exemplifies the ways in which
the romance of travel, the fervour of evangelicalism and the
earnest didacticism of the schoolroom story could combine within
a single narrative.

Early on the following morning Adelaide was seated at her window quietly reading, when a gentle tap at the door was followed by the entrance of the little Olga.

'I hope I do not derange you, mademoiselle?' said she, as she advanced.

'Do not what, my love?' said Adelaide gently, as she drew the child towards her.

'I hope I don't derange you,' repeated Olga, looking disturbed as she saw that she was not quite understood. *'J'espère que je ne vous derange pas.'*

'Oh! I understand you now,' said Adelaide, smiling affectionately; 'you meant, I hope I don't disturb you. But do you know what you really said? – I hope I don't set you mad'; and the child, relieved from her perplexity, laughed merrily with her at the idea; but Adelaide felt that the little incident was of use to her in showing the liability of mistranslations, and that her own knowledge of English must be habitually kept up by reading the best works in that language, otherwise the constant habit of speaking and hearing other languages might cause her to lose somewhat of the purity of her own.

[. . .]

In a few minutes Adelaide was equipped for her walk, and gladly set out with her little companions to visit that celebrated Winter Palace, of which she had so often heard, and was now for the first time to see. It was within a short distance of General Chernieffsky's house, so, very speedily she was occupied in traversing its length, and admiring the magnificent building which is so every way worthy of the vast empire to which it belongs. The adjoining Hermitage, however, possessed still greater attractions for her. Here she frequently went, and in it found ample means of reaching and cultivating both the minds and hearts of her pupils. In the examination of its various treasures from time to time she was able to communicate to them such solid information, and in such a pleasing manner as gained at once their esteem and love. Nor were her lessons confined to dry facts and dates, but interspersed with such lively anecdotes, and such wise and tender dealing with the reason and affections, as rapidly ripened the many amiable qualities that now began to develop themselves in both of the children.

On one subject Adelaide's lips were to a great extent closed. She could not directly speak to them of their religious differences. Still, however, the Bible was an allowed book, which, with the full consent of their parents, she read with the children daily, and mingling it ever with earnest prayer that the teaching of God's Spirit might accompany it, she left it under his guidance to do its own work in their hearts.

E.H. Hamilton, *The English Governess in Russia* (1861), pp. 31–4.

LIFE IN THE HAREM

To her conventional heading, The English Governess in Egypt, *the redoubtable Emmeline Lott added the somewhat gratuitous sub-title,* Harem Life in Egypt and Turkey, *thus adding to the usual gratifications of the travelogue the promise of voyeuristic titillation. Appointed as instructress to the Viceroy's infant son and heir, Lott loses no opportunity to satisfy her Western readers' curiosity about life 'behind the veil' of the harem, nor to confirm their sense of complacent superiority over the 'barbarous' customs of her hosts.*

As I found it utterly impossible to adopt any regular system as to the educational surveillance of H.H. the Grand Pacha, I deemed it prudent to explain in detail to Mr B. the difficulties which I had to encounter.

The irregularity which prevailed in the domestic arrangements of the Harem had totally frustrated all my endeavours to carry out any regular system. Sometimes I received orders from the Grand Eunuch, which were issued at the caprice of H.H. the Princess Epouse, who, as a matter of course, was perfectly ignorant as to the manner adopted in Europe of training up young children, to take the Grand Pacha out walking at six o'clock in the morning; on other occasions at seven, eight, and nine o'clock. And when once the little Prince was in the gardens, it was exceedingly difficult to get him to return. His will was law; and no matter how singular and unreasonable his whims were, still he must be indulged in them.

I drew up a scheme for his education, and endeavoured to obtain H.H. the Viceroy's sanction to its execution; but that Prince explained to me that he did not wish the Prince to be taught from books or toys, as he would pick up English quickly enough by being constantly with me; so that I abandoned all idea of educational training.

Then I explained to Mr. B. the numerous degradations to which I was subjected, and called his attention to the fact that I was unprovided with either chairs or tables; that I was obliged to use my trunks as substitutes for such necessaries, which were liable to, and actually did, before I retired from His Highness's service, produce spinal complaint.

Again and again, as I had previously done, when remaining as a guest, nay I should rather add as a caged bird, under his hospitable roof, I pointed out to him that not only did I find the Arab diet so nauseous to my taste as to oblige me to live chiefly upon dry bread and a little pigeon or mutton, but that, owing to the want of more nourishing food, and especially European cooking, I found my strength gradually sinking day by day; and that the constant use of coffee, and the total deprivation of those stimulants, such as malt liquor and wine, to which I had always been accustomed, and of which it is absolutely necessary that Europeans should partake in warm countries, to counteract the hostile debilitating effects of the climate, would, I fear, soon throw me on a bed of sickness.

[. . .]

Then the very atmosphere I breathed was continually impregnated with the fumes of tobacco, into which large quantities of opium and other deleterious narcotics were infused, which so affected my constitution that my spirits began to flag, and I felt a kind of heavy languid apathy come over me, that scarcely any amount of energy on my part was able to shake off.

The irksome monotony of my daily life had produced a most unpleasant feeling in my mind. Not only had I lost much of my wonted energy, but a kind of lethargy seemed to have crept over me; a most undefinable reluctance to move about had imperceptibly gained ascendancy over my actions; – to walk, to speak (and here I must not forget to mention that my voice had become extremely feeble) – to apply myself to drawing, reading, or, in fact, to make the slightest exertion of any kind whatever, had become absolutely irksome to me.

It was not the feeling of what we Europeans call *ennui* which I experienced, for that sensation can always be shook off by a little moral courage and energy; but it was a state bordering on that frightful melancholy, that must, if not dispelled, engender insanity. And my experience of such feelings is not to be wondered at, if my position in the Harem is thoroughly examined.

[. . .]

One day, when it was too hot for the Prince to take his usual morning walk in the garden, I was playing with him at football, the ball being a middle-sized India one, enclosed in net-work; the hangings of the doors being looped back to admit of a free circulation of air. His Highness happened to kick it with rather more force than usual, it bounded into the corridor, and rolled into a room, the door of which I had never seen open before, and disappeared.

The Prince followed in pursuit; but hearing him halloo out, I hastened to his assistance, and, entering the unexplored chamber, I found that the tails of his little coat had been caught in the leg of a Broadwood's grand piano. I instantly liberated the little captive, who, as soon as he had snatched up the ball, threw it into my hands, which were extended to catch it, and proceeded (as he was exceedingly curious) to examine every nook and corner of that room, which was to him an undiscovered region.

Hand-in-hand, we proceeded to take an inventory of the miscellaneous articles which were huddled up together in that 'Old Antique and Modern Curiosity Shop.' I cannot do better than compare it to the show-room of an extensive furniture-warehouse, with half-a-dozen parlours, of Wardour-street *vertù* dealers.

There we found beautifully-executed full-length portraits of her Majesty the Queen, the late Prince Consort, Napoleon III, the Empress Eugenie, and many other of the crowned heads of Europe; elegant gilt time-pieces, large bulky rolls of handsome carpet, marqueterie tables, spring easy-chairs, sofas, ornaments for mantelpieces of the most costly description.

[. . .]

It was a very large apartment (not in the Harem) and happened to be open on that day, as H.H. the Viceroy's *Tchiboukdji* was standing there, while several slaves were dusting it. I then determined to ask H.H. the Viceroy, when an opportunity offered, to allow me to have the furniture which was in it (for therein I had found everything that even a European lady of rank could desire to make her rooms comfortable) placed in the rooms above it, which would have enabled me to keep H.H. the Prince apart from the host of slaves, whose disgusting ways tended to counteract my best endeavours to bring him up in European habits and manners.

But, most unfortunately, our sudden departure for Alexandria prevented me from carrying out that *beau projet*, as also did my subsequent illness at Constantinople, which obliged me to repair to Europe. I never again returned to the Harem, for which I was not sorry.

Emmeline Lott, *The English Governess in Egypt* (1866), Vol. I, pp. 196–200, 297–300.

COMPARATIVE GEOGRAPHY

Anna Leonowens, whose famous introduction to the court of Siam we witnessed in Chapter 1, likewise found much to amaze and alarm in the manners and customs of her employers. According to

Leonowens, her early fear of the king and his exasperation with
her settled into mutual respect. Like Emmeline Lott's, Leonowens'
narrative seldom forsakes an opportunity to belittle her royal host
or to demonstrate the ignorance of her many charges. Unlike Lott,
however, Leonowens occasionally betrays a healthy consciousness
of the absurdity of her own position and pretensions.

The studies that took the most absolute possession of the fervid Eastern imaginations of my pupils were geography and astronomy. But each had his or her own idea about the form of the earth, and it needed no small amount of patient repetition to convince them that it was neither flat nor square, but round.

The only map – and a very ancient one it was – which they had ever seen was one drawn and painted about a century before, by a Siamese who was thought to possess great scientific and literary attainments.

This map was five feet long by three wide; in the centre was a great patch of red, and above it a small patch of green. On the part painted red – which was intended to represent Siam – was pasted a comical-looking human figure, cut out of silver paper, with a huge pitchfork in one hand and an orange in the other. There was a crown on the head and spurs on the heels, and the sun was shining over all. The legs, which were of miserably thin dimensions, met sympathetically at the knees. And this cadaverous-looking creature was meant for the king of Siam – indicating that so vast were his strength and power that they extended from one end of his dominions to the other. [. . .] My simple pupils knew just so much as this map taught them, and no more. Burmah on the north, and Siam on the south, and the sea all around – this was the world to them.

But of their celestial geography they could tell me a host of interesting particulars, all of which they would relate with the accuracy and picturesque vividness of a fairy tale [. . .]

I soon found that my pupils were in some respects much wiser than I, and thenceforth we exchanged thoughts and ideas. I gave them sound realities in return for their poetic illusions and chimeras, which had for me a certain charm and a great deal of odd reasonableness, for it was their way of explaining the incomprehensible.

When a large English map and globes of the celestial and terrestrial spheres arrived, they created quite a sensation in the ancient temple of the 'Mothers of the Free'. His Majesty caused the map to be set in a massive gold frame, and placed it with the globes on ponderously gilt supporters in the very middle of the temple, and for nine days crowds of women came to be instructed in the sciences of geography and astronomy, so that I found my hands quite full. It was hard for them to see Siam reduced to a mere speck on the great globe, but there was some consolation in the fact that England occupied even a smaller space.

Anna H. Leonowens, *Siamese Harem Life* (1952, first published 1873), pp. 197–9.

CHAPTER 6

SEX, SECRETS AND SUBTERFUGE: FANTASIES OF THE GOVERNESS

By 1759, according to an entry in the *Oxford English Dictionary*, 'governess' was the preferred epithet for a female teacher because 'mistress' – the feminine equivalent of the commonplace 'master' – 'has a vulgar sound with it'. It is quite possible that the term 'governess' prevailed in the nineteenth century because it demarcated the resident lady teacher from, on the one hand, the 'mistress of the house', and on the other, the derogatory and salacious connotations attached to 'having a mistress'. As Chapter 3 revealed, part of the difficulty of the governess's lot was her status as an unmarried, unchaperoned lady working outside her father's house. This involved her in the twin dangers of being exposed to unwanted attentions (from the fathers, uncles, sons or menservants of the establishment) and of appearing to be a loose sexual cannon.

As readers may have noticed, the mid-century debate about the 'Governess Question' is largely silent about her potential as a marriage partner, as a possible mother, as a sexual subject, or indeed as a subject of desire of any kind. Of course the whole point of the 'rescue' movement was to portray a constituency of women destined, through no fault or wish of their own, to remain unmarried, and who therefore needed forms of provision that would not threaten the norms of the family and of heterosexuality. Yet throughout the century there seems something overemphatic about the public image of the governess as 'spinster', as 'redundant' or 'surplus': as if she were a sort of third sex beyond the pale

Fig. 36 'Considerate – Very!' (*Punch*, 1864)

of conventional expectations. The cliché of the dried-up, sour, ugly, 'spinsterish' governess is ubiquitous in Victorian culture. Yet, as Kathryn Hughes suggests (1993, p. 118), there is no reliable evidence, and little likelihood, that governesses were any more or less physically attractive than any other sample of the population. It was unusual, but not unheard-of, for a woman – *Emma*'s fictional Miss Taylor comes to mind, but one might adduce Mary Cowden Clarke, or Mary Paley Marshall's Fräulein (Chapter 2) – to enter governessing only to marry out of it, relatively straightforwardly, as the opportunity arose. Nor can the reluctance to ascribe a sexual subjectivity to the governess be attributed solely to Victorian prudery or squeamishness. The debate about girls' education, after all, returned incessantly to the possible effects of too much learning on their reproductive capacity and marriageability. What then was at stake in the 'sexless' image of the governess?

A key factor, of course, was the need to assuage public anxiety about the presence of single, middle-class women at the heart of the bourgeois domestic idyll. As Jeanne Peterson has pointed out, even the usually frank body of advice literature is curiously reticent about the relationship between the resident governess and the paterfamilias (1972, p. 14). Between the lines, however, we witness the governess treading a tightrope between displaying her accomplishments and showing them off; between achieving propriety, and good taste in dress, manners and conversation, and appearing *too* well-dressed, *too* charming, *too* accommodating.

Another factor in the 'de-sexing' of the governess may have been her proximity to the maternal role, in an era when the idea of childhood 'purity' was in the ascendant. One cannot ignore, however, the erotic currents that eddy around the idea of childlike innocence in Victorian culture. As Henry James's novella *The Turn of the Screw* (1898) so chillingly suggests, an image of 'sexlessness' – whether in children or their carers – is quite as laborious to build as one of 'sexiness', and often draws on the same unconscious fears and urges.

This dynamic goes some way to explaining one of the most striking contradictions in the Victorian idea of the governess: that a *political* insistence on her non-sexual nature coincided, in popular and literary culture, with rampant fantasies about her secret desires. Hence the multitude of romantic heroines who, following Jane Eyre, are rescued from their sad fate by the fortunate intervention of a wealthy Rochester. Hence, too, the ranks of predatory *femmes fatales* and counterfeit governesses who, often under assumed names and in heavy disguise, attempt to erase their past misfortunes or misdeeds by advertising themselves as governesses and smuggling themselves into the apparent sanctuary of another family.

This is how the governess frequently appears in the pages of mid-century novels of sensation, and later in melodrama and even farce: as a fraudulent interloper whom the forces of justice will ultimately expose. Needless to say, however, the governess's sexual aura varied according to the genre in which she found herself. In the ever-increasing volume of

" *If you are hurt and want help, sir, I can fetch someone.'*

Fig. 37 Jane Eyre meets the mysterious master of Thornfield.

179

popular fiction for young girls, she figured as a Cinderella or Snow-White character: triumphing over adversity, homesickness and penury only to be swept off her dainty feet by an unsuspected admirer. In travel writing and adventure stories she might borrow something of the exotic flavour of the orientalized harem, while in memoirs and autobiographies of the Victorian period she often towered over upper-middle-class childhood as the embodiment of reassuring strictness and exciting power. At the murky edges of 'respectable' literature she is to be found palpitating with frustrated lust, harbouring wicked designs, or administering sadistic floggings at the drop of a hat.

By the 1890s, in fact, the term 'governess' was being freely used as part of the vocabulary of sexual obscenity. In the resolutely puerile world of Victorian pornography, it usually evoked the birch-wielding figure of the dominatrix. So entrenched was flagellation in the Victorian pornographic repertoire, however, that 'governess' became virtually a synonym for 'cheap and sexually available'. A typical article in the notorious journal *The Pearl*, for instance, advocated starting a club 'where at least 20 pretty governesses would be engaged at salaries of £100 per annum; there would be French, English, German, Russian, Italian, and even Zulu and Hottentots, so as to assimilate to every variety of taste. These ladies would accommodate the members whenever they might visit the club, and everything in the shape of dress and generous living and indulgence would be extended to these houris, to make them as agreeable as possible.' (*The Pearl*, 1880, pp. 186–7)

For all the efforts of Victorian philanthropists and advice-writers to keep 'governessing' free from sexual taint, the term gradually acquired dubious connotations. Ironically, *The Lady* reported in 1890 that lady teachers were choosing to call themselves 'mistresses' since the term 'governess' had fallen into disrepute ('Robbing Governesses', 1890, p. 235).

THE OBJECT OF PREJUDICE

Mary Maurice, whose reforming efforts we observed in Chapter 4, was one of several sisters variously involved in private teaching, and was thus supremely conscious of the fragility of the governess's reputation. Here she sums up many of the recurrent themes of this chapter: the suspicion in which the governess was held; her unenviable task of policing the purity of children and its openness to abuse; the temptation to deception and fraud that accompanied her position of trust and authority in the house; the temptation, too, to insinuate herself into the hearts – and pockets – of her employers.

It cannot be denied that there is a strong prejudice against governesses, particularly in the minds of men, and the reasons for this dislike we must not shrink from pointing out.

Frightful instances have been discovered in which she, to whom the care of the young has been entrusted, instead of guarding their minds in innocence and purity, has become their corrupter – she has been the first to lead and to initiate into sin, to suggest and carry on intrigues, and finally to be the instrument of destroying the peace of families. Very many instances, alas! are known in which habits of intemperance have been habitual, and others in which pilfering and theft have been practised to a great extent – and we must rank under the same description those who indulge in reckless habits of expenditure, with the certainty of being unable to repay what they purchase. Does this deserve a milder name than swindling?

These are the grosser forms of sin which have been generally concealed from public notice for the reasons before assigned – but none of the cases are imaginary

Fig. 38 Even an otherwise unprepossessing governess could, through her playing, inspire the imagination.

ones, and they are but too well known in the circles amongst which they occurred. In some instances again, the love of admiration has led the governess to try and make herself necessary to the comfort of the father of the family in which she resided, and by delicate and unnoticed flattery gradually to gain her point, to the disparagement of the mother, and the destruction of mutual happiness. When the latter was homely, or occupied with domestic cares, opportunity was found to bring forward attractive accomplishments, or by sedulous attentions to supply her lack of them; or the sons were in some instances objects of notice and flirtation, or when occasion offered, visitors at the house.

This kind of conduct has led to the inquiry, which is frequently made before engaging an instructress, 'Is she handsome or attractive?' If so, it is conclusive against her.

[Mary Maurice], *Governess Life: Its Trials, Duties and Encouragements* (1849), pp. 14–15.

BY HONOUR BOUND

Despite the fact that marriage was virtually the only hope of long-term security for the working governess – and even the most fervent advocates of self-dependence and fortitude for governesses found their imagination failing and their stirring tones faltering when they addressed her prospects on retirement – her position of dependence precluded the least suggestion of romantic opportunism. Commentators and gossips were only too eager to inflate occasional instances of indiscretion or flirting into full-blown condemnation of governesses as a class. As Emily Peart indicates, schooling herself in passivity and living in hope-against-hope were the only respectable options for a resident teacher who aspired to a home of her own.

How constantly you hear it said, 'Mrs — has a great objection to having a governess in the house;' and no wonder she has, poor woman! when she is conscious that her husband regards her with serene

Mamma. "Now go and say Good-night to your Governess, like a good little girl, and give her a Kiss."
Little Puss. "I'll say Good-night, but I won't give her a Kiss."
Mamma. "That's naughty! Why won't you give her a Kiss?"
Little Puss. "Because she slaps people's Faces when they try to Kiss her."
Mamma. "Now, don't talk Nonsense; but do as You're told."
Little Puss. "Well, Mummy, if you don't believe Me,——*ask Papa!*"   [*Tableau*

Fig. 39 'Kissing the Governess.' (*Punch*, 1900)

indifference, and would only be too willing to have a little pleasanter society than hers is ever likely to be to him again. How often will mothers of grown-up sons declare vehemently that they would not have a governess in the house for the world! How often will wives and mothers – good, sensible women, who have neither indifferent husbands nor grown-up sons – do everything they can, and with enough reason too, rather than run the risk of taking a lady into the house as a teacher! and when they are obliged to do so, with how much distance and coldness will they treat her, and with what guarded familiarity, lest she should forget her place, or any unpleasantness should ensue! And all this is richly deserved, and just the result of the conduct of many governesses. How many are the cases where the peace of families has been destroyed, or, at least, results have ensued the very last that might have been desired! Is it any wonder, then, that objections, for which there is no ground, are raised and felt against governesses utterly undeserving of them? It is for you to guard most jealously your name against the faintest suspicion of designs, or manoeuvring, or anything else which wears the appearance of endeavouring to secure a settlement, or entrap a husband among those with whom you live. Can you endure the thought of so doing? Whatever be your position or your sufferings – and they may be no light matter – there is one possession left you, which no other hand than your own can throw away, and that is your self-respect. Lose *this*, count it a thing of small value, and you are miserable indeed. Whatever the daily annoyances of your present life, whatever the stinging memories of the past, whatever the crushing fears for the future, whatever terrors a lonely, dependent, needy old age presents, do not mar the beauty of your womanhood by stirring a finger, by taking a step, by fashioning a circumstance with the view of gaining a husband and a home. If marriage comes to you, as it ought to come, if it ever come at all, unsought and unplanned for, rejoice that God is giving you a very faint semblance of the home above, in the peace and love of a home here; but a thousand times rather live and die a pitied, 'poor-thinged' old maid, than be a wife, conscious that her husband is but the ably-earned result of her own successful scheming.

[Emily Peart], *A Book for Governesses, by One of Them* (1869), pp. 99–102.

MISS MARKS HAS HYSTERICS

The 'poor-thinging' of 'old maids' was an occupational hazard for most governesses of the Victorian era. In memoirs, novels, paintings, engravings and cartoons she appears more or less dissatisfied, more or less drab. Edmund Gosse's fictionalized portrait of his childhood among the Plymouth Brethren, a strict dissenting sect, introduces his governess, 'Miss Marks', as a prime example of the race of spinsters: 'She was tall, rather gaunt, with high cheek-bones; her teeth were prominent and very white; her eyes were china-blue, and were always absolutely fixed, wide open, on the person she spoke to; her nose was inclined to be red at the tip. She had a kind, hearty, sharp mode of talking, but did not exercise it much, being on the whole taciturn. She was bustling and nervous, not particularly refined, not quite, I imagine, what is called "a lady."' Miss Marks, in other words, comes straight out of the Punch *gallery of governesses: a 'grotesque personage . . . a mixture of Mrs Pipchin and Miss Sally Brass'. (1907, pp. 106–7) For all that, Gosse's portrait is one of the more sympathetic pictures of the governess as reluctant old maid. Though neither intelligent nor graceful, Miss Marks is portrayed as good, honest and dutiful, and as an important figure in the life of a lonely, motherless boy. Her own yearning for love, however, whether it finds an outlet in a 'romantic friendship' with another woman, or, as here, cleaves fruitlessly to her widowed employer, excites both curiosity and mild derision in her pupil, who takes a malicious pleasure in bringing her frustrations to a head.*

Just before Christmas, on a piercing night of frost, my Father brought to us his bride. The smartening up of the house, the new furniture, the removal of my own possessions to a private bed-room, the wedding-gifts of the 'saints', all these things paled in interest before the fact that Miss Marks had made a 'scene', in the course of the afternoon. I was dancing about the drawing-room, and was saying: 'Oh! I am so glad my new Mamma is coming,' when Miss Marks called out, in an unnatural voice, 'Oh! you cruel child.' I stopped in amazement and stared at her, whereupon she threw prudence to the winds, and moaned: 'I once thought I should be your dear mamma.' I was simply stupefied, and I expressed my horror in terms that were clear and strong. Thereupon Miss Marks had a wild fit of hysterics, while I looked on, wholly unsympathetic and still deeply affronted. She was right; I was cruel, alas! but then, what a silly woman she had been! The consequence was that she withdrew in a moist and quivering condition to her boudoir, where she had locked herself in when I, all smiles and caresses, was welcoming the bride and bridegroom on the doorstep as politely as if I had been a valued old family retainer.

Edmund Gosse, *Father and Son: A Study of Two Temperaments* (1907), pp. 251–2.

FURTIVE LOOKS, ROMANTIC BOOKS

*The assumption that a governess's fantasies must be foolish and
must remain unfulfilled rendered them superficially safe, and
hence an alluring focus for the literary imagination. Though
drawing on many of the truisms of the 'plight of the governess' –
her midway position in the household, her ambiguous class status,
her sensitivity to insult – the Revd Frederick Orde Ward's
sentimental tribute to 'The Nursery Governess' relies for its
sensual effect on two sets of fantasies: the supposed cuteness of
childhood on the one hand and the heightened sexual vulnerability
of the young governess on the other. The result is a curious
mixture of avuncular affection and voyeurism.*

The Nursery Governess

On the threshold of two lands,
Joining both with useful hands
Trained to bring in perfect order
From the rule of chaos wild,
Here a wardrobe, there a child,
But a tenant of the border;
Though she does no duty ill,
And her fingers have a skill
Not to be attained by money,
Conscious of a secret might
She, who craves a bolder flight,
Longs for Canaan's milk and honey.

Half a servant, half a queen,
And two jarring worlds between,
Still she looks across like Moses
From the height of labour wrought,
On the wings of wistful thought,
To the realm of bliss and roses;

In her little sphere of frocks,
Pinafores and pretty socks,
Mabel five years old and fervent
And yet younger Maude she sways,
On first lessons' pictured ways,
Half a queen and half a servant.

Sensitive and shy and proud,
Like a star behind a cloud,
For a second rays revealing
Of an orb without a mote,
Which a careless eye would note,
Then again its light concealing;
Sometimes from a girlish dream,
Not devoid of fruit and cream,
Up she starts and goes forth brisker,
To retire within her print,
At the very faintest hint
Of an aggravating whisker.

Nurse admires her, calls her smart,
Keeps for her the crispest tart,
And employs her clever needle
For that bonnet of gay straw,
Which inspires a deeper awe
Than the cocked hat of the beadle;
Baker gives her furtive looks,
Butcher reads romantic books
And for her his fatling slaughters;
Their despair she does not guess,
If a nursery governess
Yet the flower of England's daughters.

Revd Frederick William Orde Ward, 'The Nursery Governess' in
Confessions of a Poet (1894), pp. 231–2.

THE ROMANCE OF THE NURSERY AND THE POETRY OF THE SCHOOLROOM

Of course, a piece of whimsy such as the Revd Ward's poem depends for its air of freshness and naïvety on the stability and security of certain cherished assumptions: that children really are innocent; that the governess's secret dreams are harmless, and that neither butcher, nor baker, nor clergyman for that matter, would dream of acting on their impulses. Henry James's extraordinary novella The Turn of the Screw *– ghost story or psychological thriller depending on your point of view – gains its uncanny power from the suggestion that one or other of these nostrums has been violated. Employed by an absentee guardian to take sole charge of two children, James's governess-narrator is haunted by the figure of her predecessor, the late Miss Jessel, who, in collusion with the vicious manservant Quint, also deceased, had exercised a pernicious and exclusive influence on the two children. Miles and Flora, however, appear neither tainted nor traumatized by their experience. Miles has been mysteriously expelled from boarding school, but the new governess finds herself disarmed by her enchanting pupils, and unable to suspect them of the least harm. In this passage, however, the effort to sustain her belief in them is beginning to tell.*

My charming work was just my life with Miles and Flora, and through nothing could I so like it as through feeling that to throw myself into it was to throw myself out of my trouble. The attraction of my small charges was a constant joy, leading me to wonder afresh at the vanity of my original fears, the distaste I had begun by entertaining for the probable grey prose of my office. There was to be no grey prose, it appeared, and no long grind; so how could work not be charming that presented itself as daily beauty? It was all the romance of the nursery and the poetry of the schoolroom. I don't mean by this of course that we studied only fiction and verse; I mean that I can express no otherwise the sort of interest my companions inspired. How can I describe that except by saying that instead of growing deadly used to them – and it's a marvel for a governess: I call the sisterhood to witness! – I made constant fresh discoveries. There was one direction, assuredly, in which these discoveries stopped: deep obscurity continued to cover the region of the boy's conduct at school. It had been promptly given me, I have noted, to face that mystery without a pang. Perhaps even it would be nearer the truth to say that – without a word – he himself had cleared it up. He had made the whole charge absurd. My conclusion bloomed there with the real rose-flush of his innocence: he was only too fine and fair for the little horrid unclean school-world, and he had paid a price for it.

[. . .]

Both the children had a gentleness – it was their only fault, and it never made Miles a muff – that kept them (how shall I express it?) almost impersonal and certainly quite unpunishable. They were like those cherubs of the anecdote who had – morally at any rate – nothing to whack! I remember feeling with Miles in especial as if he had had, as it were, nothing to call even an infinitesimal history. We expect of a small child scant enough 'antecendents', but there was in this beautiful little boy something extraordinarily sensitive, yet extraordinarily happy, that, more than in any creature of his age I have seen, struck me as beginning anew each day. He had never for a second suffered. I took this as a direct disproof of his having really been chastised. If he had been wicked he would have 'caught' it, and I should have caught it by the rebound – I should have found the trace, should have felt the wound and the dishonour. I could reconstitute nothing at all, and he was therefore an angel. He never spoke of his school, never mentioned a comrade or a master; and I, for my part, was quite too much disgusted to allude to them. Of course I was under the spell, and the wonderful part is that, even at the time, I perfectly knew I was. But I gave myself up to it; it was an antidote to any pain, and I had more pains than one. I was in receipt in these days of disturbing letters from home, where things were not going well. But with this joy of my children what things in the world mattered? That was the question I used to put to my scrappy retirements. I was dazzled by their loveliness.

Henry James, *The Turn of the Screw* (1898, reprinted 1987),
pp. 167–8.

A GOVERNESS PSYCHOANALYSED

*Many historians have noted the scarcity of surviving primary
evidence about the sexual aspirations and experiences of real, as
distinct from fictional or fictionalized, governesses in the
nineteenth century. Sigmund Freud's case history of 'Miss Lucy R.
(Aged 30)', an English governess working in Vienna in the 1890s,
is a rare exception. Finding that conventional medicine did not
alleviate her symptoms – loss of appetite, heaviness in the head,
fatigue, low spirits, and disturbances to her sense of smell – she
consulted Freud in 1892. His account of their subsequent meetings
and her apparent cure offers a fascinating glimpse of the hopes
and fears of a 'real life' governess.*

*Lucy R.'s recurrent sensation of the 'smell of burnt pudding' is
eventually found to originate in a scene in which her secret love
for her employer, a widower, and her situation as employee and
dependent, have come into conflict. However this also turns out to
mask another set of sense-memories: the smell of cigar smoke, and
the sight of her employer's chief accountant kissing her pupils on
the mouth – to their father's disgust and outrage. It becomes clear
that Lucy feels implicated in, and certainly is being blamed for,
actions and events over which she has no control. Freud takes up
the story.*

And now, under the pressure of my hand, the memory of a third and
still earlier scene emerged, which was the really operative trauma
and which had given the scene with the chief accountant its traumatic
effectiveness. It had happened a few months earlier still that a lady who
was an acquaintance of [Lucy R.'s] employer came to visit them, and on
her departure kissed the two children on the mouth. Their father, who
was present, managed to restrain himself from saying anything to the
lady, but after she had gone, his fury burst upon the head of the unlucky
governess. He said he held her responsible if anyone kissed the children
on the mouth, that it was her duty not to permit it and that she was
guilty of a dereliction of duty if she allowed it; if it ever happened again

he would entrust his children's upbringing to other hands. This had happened at a time when she still thought he loved her, and was expecting a repetition of their first friendly talk. The scene had crushed her hopes. She had said to herself: 'If he can fly out at me like this and make such threats over such a trivial matter, and one for which, moreover, I am not in the least responsible, I must have made a mistake. He can never have had any warm feelings for me, or they would have taught him to treat me with more consideration.'

[. . .]

After this last analysis, when, two days later, Miss Lucy visited me once more, I could not help asking her what had happened to make her so happy. [. . .] 'Nothing has happened. It's just that you don't know me. You have only seen me ill and depressed. I'm always cheerful as a rule. When I woke yesterday morning the weight was no longer on my mind, and since then I have felt well.' – 'And what do you think of your prospects in the house?' – 'I am quite clear on the subject. I know I have none, and I shan't make myself unhappy over it.' – 'And will you get on all right with the servants now?' 'I think my own oversensitiveness was responsible for most of that.' – 'And are you still in love with your employer?' – 'Yes, I certainly am, but that makes no difference. After all, I can have thoughts and feelings to myself.'

Sigmund Freud, 'Miss Lucy R.', (first published in German 1895, 1988), pp. 185–6.

THE FASCINATING MISS GWILT

Freud's 'Lucy R.' provides a tantalizing insight into the possible psychic costs of governessing, as well as into the resilience of one particular incumbent. Even here, however, we must be wary of deducing too much from slight and tendentious evidence. Our own interpretation of 'Lucy's' story is inevitably coloured by the very theories of hysteria it helped to generate. Furthermore, Freud notoriously drew on the resources of fiction when reconstructing his analyses for publication.

Fig. 40 The moth and the candle: Miss Gwilt in seductive mood.

*The secretive, turbulent inner life of the governess had been a
favourite resource of the novelists since the publication of
Charlotte and Anne Brontë's best-loved works in the late 1840s.
A vogue for 'novels of sensation' in the 1860s accentuated her
enigmatic and alluring image. The seductive, dangerous heroines of
Mrs Henry Wood's best-selling* East Lynne *(1861) and Mary
Elizabeth Braddon's* Lady Audley's Secret *(1862) both resorted to
governessing to obscure their murky pasts, while the portrait of the
governess as devious adventuress was perfected by Wilkie Collins
in* Armadale's *scheming Miss Gwilt (1866). Novels of sensation
lent themselves to many popular versions for the stage. Here we
sample one of several theatrical versions of Collins's* Armadale.

SCENE. –The interior of the fishing-house at Thorpe-Ambrose,
divided by a vertical partition – with a door in it – into two rooms of
unequal size. The larger of the two opens on a terrace and verandah

at the back of the stage, commanding a view of a sheet of water. This room is fitted up as a museum, and is decorated with Indian and Chinese curiosities, fishing implements, ancient and modern weapons, models of ships and boats, and in a prominent place a model of a schooner-yacht.

The smaller room (fitted up as a reading room) is entered by a door in the partition. The upper part of the door is of glass, covered by a curtain on the side of the reading-room. Newspapers, periodicals, and writing materials are on the table.

[. . .]

At the rise of the curtain MAJOR MILROY, MISS MILROY, and MISS GWILT are discovered in the museum. MISS GWILT is seated at one end of the room making a water-colour drawing of a Chinese figure. The MAJOR stands looking over her. MISS MILROY is alone at the opposite end of the room, examining a book of engravings.

Major M: Miss Gwilt, you are the most universally-gifted person I have ever met with. If my reckoning is right, you have been a resident in our family for something like three weeks. I declare hardly a day has passed without our finding some fresh accomplishment of yours to admire! Neelie! why don't you come and look at Miss Gwilt's drawing?

Miss M: I am looking at the works of Raphael, papa. Perhaps I may be excused if I have no admiration to spare, even for Miss Gwilt.

Miss G: I am charmed to find, my dear, that you are making some progress in your knowledge of art. It is something to have discovered that Raphael was a better painter than I am!

[. . .]

Major M: [. . .] (*Looks over* MISS GWILT's *shoulder*.) How well you are getting on with your drawing, Miss Gwilt! How well you do everything! Were you educated in England?

Miss G: Partly in England and partly in France. My poor mother's small resources were heavily taxed, Major, for my sake.

Major M: The sacrifice has not been without its reward, Miss Gwilt. It has made you the accomplished woman you are now.

Miss G: (*smiling sadly*). It has done more than that. It has made me feel keenly my dependent position in the world. I have had the training of a lady – for the life of a servant! My mind has been cultivated, my tastes have been refined – and all for what? To see people without mind and without taste prosperous and happy – to find my poverty degrading all that is highest and best in me to the level of something to sell, something which the insolence of wealth can purchase on its own terms. Don't think me ungrateful! I am speaking of the time before you knew me. Will the day ever come when I shall deserve your kindness? Shall I stay with you long enough to win a sister's place in my pupil's heart?

Miss M: You are very good, Miss Gwilt. If you stayed here a hundred years I should never forget you were my governess!

Major M: Neelie, that is a very improper answer to make to Miss Gwilt.

Miss G: (*to the* MAJOR:). Pray don't notice it! *You* understand me, don't you?

Major M: I understand, and thank you. It is really a question, Miss Gwilt – at your age and with your attractions – whether I have any right to keep you buried in this obscure place. A brilliant future may be awaiting you.

Miss G: (*going on with her drawing*). You are very kind, Major. I have no faith in the future.

Major M: No faith in the future! Your worthy friend, Dr Downward, doesn't take *that* view of your prospects, I am sure. I was sorry he had to hurry back to London on the day when he introduced you to us. Is there any chance of our soon seeing the Doctor again?

Miss G: Yes. He speaks of paying another visit to his patient in Norfolk, and of coming here afterwards to see me in my new home.

Major M: I am delighted to hear it. When you have told the good Doctor all your news, I may have something to tell him on my side in which your interests are concerned. (*Smiling, and lowering his voice.*) There are younger men than I am in this neighbourhood who have the taste to admire you. There is one young gentleman whose daily walks take him wonderfully often in the direction of my cottage. Aha! you understand me *now*?

Miss G: (aside in alarm). Does he mean Midwinter?

Miss M: (aside in alarm). Does he mean Allan?

Major M: Look into the future, Miss Gwilt, and you may see the lady who is soon to be mistress of this great estate.

> *(He walks up the stage towards the door.)*

Miss G: (aside with an air of relief). He means Armadale!

[. . .]

(THE MAJOR *and* MISS M. *go out.* MISS G. *puts aside her drawing materials, rises, and walks irritably up and down the room.)*

Miss G: My position becomes more insupportable every day. The insolence of Miss Milroy; the blindness of her father to what is going on under his own eyes; the utter impossibility of my marrying Armadale, as Doctor Downward had planned – everything is at cross purposes – everything is going wrong! I wish I was hundreds of miles from this place! I wish I had been left dead at the bottom of the river! *(Pauses.)* Strange! Whenever I am most reckless, whenever I am most wretched now – the thought of that friend of Armadale's comes and softens me. Midwinter! I am thinking of Midwinter again! Have I a heart still left? and has that man touched it?

(MIDWINTER *appears at the verandah.)*

Mid: Miss Gwilt, may I hope that I am not intruding on you? I have something to tell you this morning, and I hardly know how to approach the subject.

Miss G: (smiling). Am I so very terrible?

Mid: You are the kindest and gentlest of women!

Miss G: (aside). What is it that speaks to me in his voice? – what is it that looks at me in his eyes? *(To MID.)* You seem agitated. Has anything vexed you this morning?

Mid: I have parted this morning from something very precious to me. I have thought it right, in case of accidents, to destroy your letter – the only letter you have ever written to me.

Miss G: My letter? Ah, yes! I wrote to thank you for your merciful silence about me in this place. You have told nobody here that I am the woman whom you saw charged at the police-station with an attempt on her life.

Mid: As a favour to *me*, don't, pray don't, speak of it again!

Miss G: I dare not ask myself what you must think of me. I can claim your pity, and I can claim no more! (*She leaves him dejectedly, and seats herself in a corner of the room.*)

Mid: For God's sake, Miss Gwilt, believe that you inspire me with a feeling worthier of you than pity! My heart bleeds for you! my heart longs for you! (*He kneels at her feet.*) I have dared to love you! (*A pause.*) With the first love I have ever known – with the last love I shall ever feel! Have I offended you?

Wilkie Collins, *Miss Gwilt: A Drama in Five Acts* (1875), pp. 23–7.

THE PRICE OF FREEDOM

As the century went on, the relative anonymity and apparent outcast status of the governess licensed ever more convoluted plots and bizarre variations on her dark secret. Madge Wilfrey in Emma Raymond Pitman's school story, My Governess Life *(1883) finds her reputation compromised when she is persecuted by the unwanted attentions of a stranger. Only reluctantly does she reveal his real identity to her employer. Huldah Rossiter in Rosa Nouchette Carey's* Only The Governess *(1899) turns to governessing to escape from her seemingly cold, unaffectionate husband Ivan and his jealous sister Rachel. Her fault (ironically, given the myth of the predatory governess) is to have passed herself off as single, when she saw herself as definitively spoken for.*

'That man is my father, Mrs Blake!'

'When, some years ago, my father got into trouble owing to his love of gambling, he fell into the hands of the law, and suffered the penalty. I was left at home, to nurse my mother through a long illness, from which she never recovered. When she passed away, I was left alone – almost alone, a felon's daughter – to make my way in the world. Some relatives educated me, and sent me out to earn my own living as governess, seeing that I should never know again the shelter of a parent's

Fig. 41 'Dear Madge, you are in trouble!'

home. My mother was dead, my father a convict, and my only brother an exile from his native land, because he could not endure the burden of shame which lighted upon him. I have laboured diligently, as a governess; I think, Mrs Blake, you cannot say otherwise, and I hoped sincerely that my father would never find me out again. I saw him once after his return from the convict establishment, but he was so changed that I never wanted to see him more. He left England for Baden-Baden, or some other foreign town, where, according to the uncertain news we heard of him, he spent his time in billiard-saloons – of course, in subordinate positions, seeing that he could not assume the *rôle* of gentleman. Several times I have received letters from him, and of late with one object in view – to get me to go out to him. A certain share of prosperity must have attended his gambling adventures, inasmuch as he now represents to me that he has a house of his own, and needs somebody to manage it. I have such a

Fig. 42 'A Father's Degradation!'

horror of gambling, that I cannot go to Baden-Baden. *I will not*. I have disregarded his letters, and, in fact, abstained from answering them of late, hoping that he would get tired and cease to persecute me. Instead of this, however, on the morning of the fire, my father way-laid us as we were walking out at "recreation time," and recognized me in a moment. I knew him, too, and had it not been for Miss Northcroft's support, I should have fallen to the ground . . . .'

Emma Raymond Pitman, *My Governess Life* (1883), pp. 197–8.

I Had My Freedom

'In a fit of passionate anger and despair I declared that I would be Ivan's wife no longer. The terms of our separation did not satisfy me. I was still under his control, he still sent me money from time to time, and no doubt it was by his wish that Rachel wrote to me.

I determined in an evil moment, and quite heedless of consequences, that I would be free, indeed. When Mrs Selby died, leaving me a small legacy, I went to the Governesses' Registry in Harley Street – we were in London then – and entered myself on the books as Huldah Rossiter, my mother's maiden name, and there I met your dear mother.'

'Good heavens! do you mean to tell me that Madella took you without references?' and at this question a ghost of the old smile crossed the girl's lips.

'She was very easily contented; the fact is, we took a fancy to each other at the first moment. I told her I had been unfortunate; that my benefactress was dead, and had left me a small legacy, but that I had no relation to speak for me, which was perfectly true. I also told her of Aunt Kezia's death, which had thrown me on the world. She hesitated at first, but appointed a second interview, and when I saw her again, she said, to my surprise, that it was all right; a lady she knew well had been acquainted with Mrs Selby, and had heard her speak with great affection of a young lady companion. "To be sure," she continued, "my friend made one mistake, for she thought it was a young married lady, who had been separated from her husband; but, of course, that must have been a mistake; she must have meant you, my dear."'

'"She certainly meant me," was my reply, and to my intense relief, it was decided that I should come on trial as Sybil's governess. I told Mrs Chudleigh that I had never had a pupil before, but it appears she and Bee were much taken with my playing and singing, and my French accent was declared very satisfactory.'

[. . .]

'And now you know all the rest. Oh, how happy you all made me! There were times when I forgot Ivan, and felt as though I were a child again. Do not look at me in that way, Mr Chudleigh; indeed, they were both happier without me – they had each other. Ivan and his faithful Rachel' – and here she laughed a little hysterically – 'and I – I had my freedom.'

Rosa Nouchette Carey, *Only the Governess* (1899), pp. 195–6.

CHEAP AND THRILLING

*The attractive, tempestuous figure of Huldah Rossiter reminds us
that the governess's unprotected state could – from another point
of view – look like glamorous freedom from familial constraint.
Many of the governesses featured in Chapter 5 certainly partook
of this mystique. The penny novelette quoted below – purportedly
penned by its genteel heroine but more likely of less refined
provenance – combines the spicier ingredients of governess
mythology in quick succession, adding to this heady brew an
element from Victorian porn: the gratuitous flogging scene.*

On Sundays we used to attend the village church, which was about
two miles from the school; after the service some of the principal
ladies of the place would talk to us, one of them a Mrs. Thompson,
invited me to her house. I spent several pleasant evenings there; she had
a son and two daughters, Lucinda and Evelina. Her husband belonged
to the Diplomatic service, and was stationed at Constantinople, where
they intended to join him in a few weeks. She wanted to engage a
governess for her daughters, and asked me whether I thought I should
like a voyage. I replied that nothing would give me greater delight, so
she undertook to let me know some time before she intended to start; as
it was nearly the middle of summer, I anticipated a delightful voyage.

In the meantime my school life continued the same; the surrounding
country was beautiful at this period of the year. Each teacher took her
own class out walking in the afternoon; sometimes we would join the
boys' games in the playground. The most amusing hour for us was just
before bed time, when the delinquents of the day were punished in the
Matron's room; there were generally one or two who had misbehaved
themselves during the day; every offence was punished with a certain
number of strokes; Lucy Jones and I assisted the Matron by turns, the
remaining teacher taking charge of the school. The delinquent was tied
on to a chair, and there was generally a good struggle before we could
get a boy into the proper position; but when we did, we made him feel
the weight of our arms.

[En route to Constantinople, the newly appointed governess and her pupils are captured by pirates, and given over to the service of the exotic Zuleima.]

'Now, miss, next time I have any impudence from you, I shall make you smart, so you behave yourself.'

We saw nothing of the Pirate for a day or two; we were allowed on deck part of the day, but were kept principally in the cabin. After we had been on board a day, Zuleima made us all work; of course there was very little to do, but what there was she made us do. It was the second morning I think, she told me to make the beds. I said I should not. She gave me five minutes to consider whether I would obey her or not. At the end of five minutes she asked me again and I refused. The struggle then commenced; she seized me and tried to throw me down. I resisted, and my three companions came to my assistance; we had her by the arms when she stamped her foot, and almost immediately a Moorish boy rushed in and dragged Lucinda off. He threw her down and held her. Zuleima flung the rest of us off, tripped us up and dragged us into a little room adjoining the saloon. One by one she stripped us to the waist, and tying us to a pillar, flogged us with a thick strap. She reserved me till the last, and when she had finished the others, I was secured in the same manner. She then opened a drawer and took a different strap; it was about two feet long, broad, and cut into strips part of its length, with this she gave me twelve stripes; the pain was dreadful, but I was quite helpless. After that I was let down again, with a warning to be more obedient in future.

Anon., *Adventures of a Young Lady* (1880), pp. 6–14.

LADY POKINGHAM REMEMBERS

In reality, corporal punishment, especially of girls, was seldom recommended to the governess as part of her pedagogic repertoire. In fact it has frequently been argued that Victorian pornography's obsession with spanking and flogging of young women, often by sadistic governesses and schoolmistresses, had more to do with the

repressed homosexual longings of the (male) pornographer and his
readers than with recollections of actual governesses. Yet their
appearance in such unsavoury scenarios, however far-fetched and
stereotyped, cannot be ignored in so far as it formed part of the
popular imagery with which they had to contend.

Miss Birch was rather an indulgent schoolmistress, and only had to resort to personal punishment for very serious offences, which she considered might materially affect the future character of her pupils, unless thoroughly cut out of them from the first. I was nearly seven years old when I had a sudden fancy for making sketches on my slate in school. One of our governesses, Miss Pennington, was a rather crabbed and severe old girl of five-and-thirty, and particularly evoked my abilities as a caricaturist, and the sketches would be slyly passed from one to the other of us, causing considerable giggling and gross inattention to our lessons. I was infatuated and conceited with what I considered my clever drawings and several admonitions and extra tasks as punishment had no effect in checking my mischievous interruptions, until one afternoon Miss Birch had fallen asleep at her desk, and old Penn was busy with a class, when the sudden inspiration seized me to make a couple of very rude sketches; one of the old girl sitting on a chamber utensil; but the other was a rural idea of her stooping down, with her clothes up to ease herself, in a field. [. . .] Penn pounced upon it like an eagle, and carried it in triumph to Miss Birch.

[. . .]

'My young lady must smart for this, Miss Pennington,' said Miss Birch, with suddenly assumed gravity; 'she has been very troublesome lately with these impudent drawings, but this is positively obscene; if she draws one thing she will go to another. Send for Susan to bring my birch rod! I must punish her whilst my blood is warm, as I am too forgiving, and may let her off.'

I threw myself on my knees, and implored for mercy, promising 'Never, never to do anything of the kind again.'

MISS BIRCH: – 'You should have thought of the consequences before you drew such filthy pictures; the very idea of one of my young ladies being capable of such productions is horrible to me; these prurient ideas cannot be allowed to settle in your mind for an instant, if I can whip them out.'

Miss Pennington, with a grim look of satisfaction, now took me by the wrist, just as Susan, a stout, strong, fair servant girl of about twenty, appeared with what looked to me a fearful big bunch of birch twigs, neatly tied up with red velvet ribbon.

'Now, Lady Beatrice Pokingham,' said Miss Birch, 'kneel down, confess your fault, and kiss the rod,' taking the bunch from Susan's hands, and extending it to me as a queen might her sceptre to a supplicant subject.

[. . .]

With trembling hands I lifted my skirts, and was then ordered to open my drawers also; which done, they pinned up my dress and petticoats as high as my shoulders; then I was laid across a desk, and Susan stood in front of me, holding both hands, whilst old Penn and the French governess (who had just entered the schoolroom) each held one of my legs, so that I was what you might call helplessly spread-eagled.

MISS BIRCH: looking seriously round as she flourished the rod. – 'Now, all you young ladies, let this whipping be a caution to you; my Lady Beatrice richly deserves this degrading shame, for her indecent (I ought to call them obscure) sketches. Will you! will you, you troublesome, impudent little thing, ever do so again? There, there, there, I hope it will soon do you good. Ah! you may scream; there's a few more to come yet.'

The bunch of birch seemed to crash on my bare bottom with awful force; the tender skin smarted, and seemed ready to burst at every fresh cut. 'Ah! ah! oh!!! Oh, heavens! have mercy, madame. Oh! I will never do anything like it again. Ah – r – re! I can't bear it!' I screamed, kicking and struggling under every blow, so that at first they could scarcely hold me, but I was soon exhausted by my own efforts.

MISS BIRCH: – 'You can feel it a little, may it do you good, you bad little girl; if I don't check you now, the whole establishment would soon be demoralized. Ah! ha! your bottom is getting finely wealed, but I haven't done yet,' cutting away with increasing fury.

Just then I caught a glimpse of her face, which was usually pale, but now flushed with excitement, and her eyes sparkled with unwonted animation. 'Ah!' she continued, 'young ladies beware of my rod, when I do have to use it. How do you like it, Lady Beatrice? Let us all know how nice it is,' cutting my bottom and thighs deliberately at each ejaculation.

Anon., 'Lady Pokingham; Or They All Do It,' (1879), pp. 13–17.

A VERY DANGEROUS CHARACTER?

We end with a piece of governess-nonsense from the turn of the century: J.F. Vallings's 'farcical comedietta for the drawing room or school room', The New Governess. *Written for children, this light-hearted romp makes a joke of governess imagery: her suspect femininity, her social incongruence, her reputation for misconduct, her supposed gentility and 'properness'. It is salutary to imagine a late Victorian instructress, healthily sceptical of the prevalent stories about her, joining in the fun.*

Scene III

The Drawing Room. Tea Things.
Lady Swann: I wish I wasn't shy. With my years and experience it's absurd. Yet I feel a vague alarm about this governess. Miss Something – oh, Miss Summers, that is. Oh, here she is.
(*Enter* MISS SUMMERS.)
Lady S: How do you do, Miss Summers? I hope you are not tired with your journey. I'm sure you'd like some tea.
Miss S: No, thank you. I had some grog – tea, I mean, at the station; and I am as right as a trivet. I'd rather go to my room, and unpack my togs – clothes, I mean.
Lady S: (*stiffly*). Very well. And how soon shall I be able to introduce the dear children to you?
Miss S: Oh, bless the kids – children, I mean. When I've got a bit straight upstairs (aside), and had a squint around.
Lady S: Well, sit down a moment, while they're taking your luggage

upstairs. I will show you the school room. That is their nest, workshop, playground, and everything. You know it is a large room, and divided into two by a screen.

Miss S: Half and half, work and play, I suppose.

Lady S: Yes, and it has a large bow window, and a door opening directly into the garden.

Miss S: Indeed! (*excitedly*) That's splendid.

Lady S: (*surprised*). Yes, but I keep it locked now in winter time, or they'd be rollicking about the garden all day and night, and hide away at lesson time as they did from poor Miss Meek.

Miss S: Oh, it's a pity to keep it locked. I hope you'll give me the blooming key.

Lady S: (*aside*). Blooming key! I don't like this person at all. Her manner is abrupt, her language common. I shan't keep her long. But as the children are rather wild, perhaps a rough hand may be best for them.

Miss S: (*aside*). Wonder what the party thinks of me. I must mind my p's and q's. One night will be enough for the job. The pals always said I'd cheek enough for anything: and as I've always been such a ladies' man I can put on some of their little ways.

[. . .]

Scene V

Time, Night. School Room (dark).

Enter MISS SUMMERS (*holding a bag and candle*). Hush. I think they are all asleep. I've picked up a few valuables and jewels. I guess they won't forget their new governess in a hurry. They'll miss me, just about. Perhaps the genuine article will arrive today. Thanks to the intercepted letters, and that fool Eliza Ann in our pay, we've been able to work this deal at last. Three hearty cheers for the Brilliant Burglar Co., and their worthy chairman, your humble servant. We shall now be set up in business in the handsomest manner. Windsor Castle and Osborne House will soon open their doors to us: and the Crown jewels will take an airing next. But, hark! there's a knock at the front door, and a carriage. What's up now? Perhaps it is the real new governess. I'll hide behind this screen and clear out.

[*Hides.*]

Lady (to manager of Servants' Registry). "I WISH TO OBTAIN A NEW GOVERNESS."

Manager. "WELL, MADAM, YOU REMEMBER WE SUPPLIED YOU WITH ONE ONLY LAST WEEK, BUT, JUDGING BY THE REPORT WE HAVE RECEIVED, WHAT YOU REALLY NEED IS A LION-TAMER."

Fig. 43 *Punch* continued to comment on the governess regime and the problem of unruly children well into the twentieth century. This cartoon appeared in 1920.

Enter LORD SWANN (*in a dressing-gown*).

What a good thing I was sitting up reading. That must be the doctor I suppose, knocking. Better late than never. Someone did say the children were ill and wanted a doctor. But Isabel never mentioned it when I got home. I'll open the door myself and solve the mystery.

[*Exit.*]

Re-enter LORD S. *and* DETECTIVE SHARPE.

Detective S: No, my lord, I am not the doctor. Sharpe is my name, and sharp my nature, he he! I am a detective. I happen to know that your lordship (*speaking very low*) harbours a very dangerous character on your premises.

Lord S: Indeed, none of the servants? I hope not. I did hear that Henry was an advanced Radical.

Detective: No, though one female may be implicated with the chief offender. Did you receive a lady in the house to-day, purporting to be the new governess?

Lord S: Certainly, and Lady Swann told me she thought her a very brusque and ill-bred person.

Detective: Her ladyship is right. She is – ha, ha – the notorious burglar Bill Hawke. Will you show me her, or rather his, bedroom? I've come to arrest him, alive or dead. The police have already caught his mates in your park.

(*A click of a pistol is heard behind the screen.*)

Detective: Did you hear that? On to him.

(*Lord S. and he run either side of the screen. A struggle. Pistol goes off. The sound brings in Lady S. and the children.*)

Miss S: I must bid you all farewell as I am going on a holiday during her Majesty's pleasure. Pray don't forget me. I hope you will all like the real new governess.

(Curtain.)

J.F. Vallings, The New Governess: A Farcical Comedietta (1896),
pp. 8–16.

BIBLIOGRAPHY

Abdy, Maria. *Poetry, 2nd Series*. London, J. and W. Robins (for private circulation), 1838

Advertisement. *The Governess: a Repertory of Female Education*. Vol. 1, No. 6 (June 1855), p. 5

Anon. *Adventures of a Young Lady, Who Was First a Governess, and Who Afterwards Fell into the Hands of Pirates: Together with the Account of Her Escape*, London, published for the booksellers, 1880

Anon. *Eleanor's Governess*, London and Edinburgh, Gall and Inglis, 1909

Anon. *Hints to a Young Governess on Beginning a School*, London, Wertheim and Macintosh, 1857

Anon. *The Kind Governess Or: How to Make Home Happy*, Edinburgh, Nimmo, 1869

Anon. 'Lady Pokingham; or They All Do It: Giving an Account of her Luxurious Adventures, both before and after her Marriage with Lord Crim-Con,' *The Pearl*, vol. 1, no. 1 (July 1879), pp. 13–17

Anon. *A Word to a Young Governess by an Old One*, London, A.W. Bennett, 1860

Austen, Jane. *Emma*, ed. and introd. Ronald Blythe, Harmondsworth, Penguin, 1977

Baylis, Henry T. *The Rights, Duties and Relations of Domestic Servants and their Masters and Mistresses, with a Short Account of Servants' Institutions &c. and their Advantages*, 4th edition, London, C. Roworth and Sons, 1873

Bennet, George B. *The Christian Governess: A Memoir and a Selection from the Correspondence of Mrs. Sarah Bennet*, London, James Nisbet, 1862

Bicknell, Anna L. *Life in the Tuileries under the Second Empire*, London, T. Fisher Unwin, 1895

Brontë, Anne. *Agnes Grey*, ed. Hilda Marsden and Robert Inglesfield, Oxford, Clarendon, 1988

Brontë, Charlotte. *Jane Eyre*, ed. Q.D. Leavis, Harmondsworth, Penguin Classics, 1985

——. Letter from Charlotte Brontë to W.S. Williams, 12 May 1848, MS Grolier F3, Brontë Parsonage Museum, Haworth

Butler, Charles. *An Easy Guide to Geography and the Use of the Globes, For the Use of Schools and Private Instructors*, London, Thomas Dean, 1846

Cardigan and Lancastre, Countess of. *My Recollections*, London, Eveleigh Nash, 1909

Carey, Rosa Nouchette. *Only the Governess*, London, Macmillan, 1899

Chisholm, A.H. 'Elizabeth Gould, some "New" Letters', *Journal of the Royal Australian Historical Society*, vol. 49, no. 5 (January 1964), pp. 321–36

Coleridge, Sara. *Pretty Lessons in Verse for Good Children*, with some Lessons in Latin in Easy Rhyme, London, S. King, 1875

'College for Governesses,' *Punch*, 2 October 1847, p. 131

Collins, Wilkie. *Miss Gwilt: A Drama in Five Acts (altered from the Novel of Armadale)*, printed for performance in the Theatre only, 1875

——. *Armadale*, London, Smith, Elder, 1877

Cowden-Clarke, Mary. *My Long Life: An Autobiographic Sketch*, London, T. Fisher Unwin, 1896

'Daily Governesses,' *The Times*, 8 May 1852, p. 8

[Eastlake, Elizabeth.] 'Hints on the Modern Governess System,' *Fraser's Magazine*, vol. 31 (November 1844), pp. 571–83

[——.] '*Vanity Fair, Jane Eyre* and the Governesses' Benevolent Institution,' *Quarterly Review*, vol. 84 (December 1848), pp. 153–85

Elliott, Mary. *Flowers of Instruction, or, Familiar Subjects in Verse*, London, William Darton, 1820

'English Chaplain.' 'The Treatment of Governesses in France and England,' *The Times*, 18 December 1857, p. 5

Forbes, Angela. *Memories and Base Details*, London, Hutchinson, 1922

Freud, Sigmund. 'Miss Lucy R.' in Sigmund Freud and Joseph Breuer, *Three Studies on Hysteria*, ed. and tr. James and Alix Strachey, rev. ed. Angela Richards, Harmondsworth, Penguin, 1988, pp. 169–89

Gaskell, Elizabeth C. *The Life of Charlotte Brontë*, 2nd ed, 2 vols, London, Smith, Elder, 1857

Gosse, Edmund. *Father and Son: A Study of Two Temperaments*, London, William Heinemann, 1907

'Governess Abroad,' *Punch*, 4 October 1862, p. 139

'Governess Strike Wanted,' *Punch*, 3 September 1859, p. 96

'Governesses,' *The Times*, 25 March 1845, p. 5

Governesses' Benevolent Institution. *Annual Reports 1843–53*, London, Edward Brewster, 1844–54

Greg, W.R. 'Why are Women Redundant?' *National Review*, vol. 14 (April 1862), pp. 434–60

Greig, John. 'The Young Ladies' New Guide to Arithmetic' in *An Introduction to the Use of Globes for Youth of Both Sexes; Particularly Designed for Schools and Private Teachers*, London, Baldwin, Cradock and Joy, 1816

Grier, Sydney C. *His Excellency's English Governess*, Edinburgh and London, Blackwood, 1896

Hall, Mrs. S.C. *The Governess: A Tale*, London and Edinburgh, W. and R. Chambers, 1858

Hamilton, E.H. *The English Governess in Russia*, London, Nelson and Sons, 1861

Ingelow, Jean. *Studies for Stories*, London, Alexander Strahan, 1864

James, Henry. *The Turn of the Screw* in *The Aspern Papers* and *The Turn of the Screw*, ed. and introd. Anthony Curtis, Harmondsworth, Penguin, 1984, pp. 145–262

Kerr, Robert. *The Gentleman's House; Or, How to Plan English Residences from the Parsonage to the Palace; with Tables of Accommodation and Cost, and a Series of Selected Plans*, 2nd ed. (rev.), London, John Murray, 1865

Leonowens, Anna Harriette. *The English Governess at the Siamese Court: Being Recollections of Six Years in the Royal Palace at Bangkok*, Philadelphia, Porter and Coates, 1870

——. *Siamese Harem Life*, introd., Freya Stark, London, Arthur Barker, 1952

Lott, Emmeline. *The English Governess in Egypt: Harem Life in Egypt and Constantinople*, 2 vols, London, Richard Bentley, 1866

Luard, Julia. *The Childhood and Schoolroom Hours of Royal Children*, London, Groombridge, 1865

Lucy, Mary Elizabeth. *Mistress of Charlecote: The Memoirs of Mary Elizabeth Lucy*, introd. Alice Fairfax-Lucy, London, Victor Gollancz, 1987

M'Crindell, R. *The English Governess: A Tale of Real Life*, London, W.H. Dalton, 1844

Mangnall, Richmal. *Historical and Miscellaneous Questions for the Use of Young People*, London, Longman and Rees, 1800

Marshall, Mary Paley. *What I Remember*, introd. G.M. Trevelyan, Cambridge, Cambridge University Press, 1947

Martineau, Harriet. *Deerbrook*, introd. Gaby Weiner, London, Virago, 1983

Mathews, Mrs. C. *Ellinor: The Young Governess, A Moral Tale Interspersed with Historical Anecdotes &c*, York, Thomas Wilson, 1809

Maurice, Frederick Denison. 'Queen's College, London: Its Objects and Method' in *Introductory Lectures Delivered at Queen's College, London*, London, John W. Parker, 1849

[Maurice, Mary.] *Mothers and Governesses*, London, John W. Parker, 1847

[——.] *Governess Life: Its Trials, Duties and Encouragements*, London, John W. Parker, 1849

Montgomery, Florence. *Behind the Scenes in the Schoolroom: Being the Experiences of a Young Governess*, London, Macmillan, 1913

Panton, J.E. *From Kitchen to Garret: Hints for Young Householders*, London, Ward and Downey, 1888

[Parkes, Bessie Rayner, attrib.] 'The Profession of the Teacher,' *English Woman's Journal*, vol. 1, no. 1 (March 1858), pp. 1–13

[Peart, Emily.] *A Book for Governesses, by one of them*, Edinburgh, William Oliphant, 1869

Pitman, Emma Raymond. *My Governess Life*, London, Blackie and Son, 1883

'Poor Governess.' 'White Slavery,' *The Times*, 20 January 1857, p. 12

Pycroft, James. 'Your Daughter's Education' in *Englishwoman's Domestic Magazine* N.S, vol. 7 (1852), pp. 79–84

Ridout, S.F. *Letters to a Young Governess on the Principles of Education*, London, Edmund Fry, 1840

'Robbing Governesses', *The Lady*, 20 February 1890, pp. 235–7

Rossetti, Christina G. Autograph Letters to Mme. Lega-Fletcher, December 1883–October 1885, Brotherton Collection, MS B1349

Smythies, Harriet Gordon. *The Daily Governess: or Self-Dependence*, London, Hurst and Blackett, 1861

Stephen, George. *Guide to Service: The Governess*, London, Charles Knight, 1844

Thackeray, William Makepeace. *Vanity Fair: a Novel Without a Hero*, London, Bradbury and Evans, 1849

——. *The Newcomes: Memoirs of a Most Respectable Family*, introd. Lady Ritchie, London, Smith, Elder, 1911

Thomson, Anthony F. *The English Schoolroom; or Thoughts on Private Tuition, Practical and Suggestive*, London, Sampson Low, Son, and Marston, 1865

'To The Editor,' *The Times*, 28 October 1844, p. 8

Vallings, J.F. *The New Governess: A Farcical Comedietta for the Drawing Room or School Room*, London, A.D. Innes, 1896

Walford, Lucy Bethia. *Recollections of a Scottish Novelist*, Buckinghamshire, Kylin Press, 1984

'Wanted A Governess,' *The Times*, 16 April 1849, p. 8

Ward, Frederick William Orde. *Confessions of a Poet*, London, Hutchinson, 1894

Weeton, Ellen. *Miss Weeton's Journal of a Governess*, introd. J.J. Bagley, 2 vols, Newton Abbot, David and Charles, 1969

Wells, Helena. *Letters on Subjects of Importance to the Happiness of Young Females*, London: L. Peacock, 1799.

Wood, Mary Bristow. *The Entomological Researcher: or, Dialogues between a Governess and her Pupil*, London, William Edward Painter, 1845

Yonge, Charlotte M. *Womankind*, London, Mozley and Smith, 1876

——. *Hopes and Fears*, London, Macmillan, 1899

Further Reading

Beatty, J.W. *The Story of the Governesses' Benevolent Society*, printed for private circulation, 1962

Clarke, Patricia. *The Governesses: Letters from the Colonies, 1862–1882*, London, etc., Allen and Unwin, 1985

Gérin, Winifred. *Anne Thackeray Ritchie: A Biography*, Oxford, OUP, 1981

Horn, Pamela. 'The Victorian Governess,' *History of Education*, vol. 18, no. 4 (1989), pp. 333–44

——. *Ladies of the Manor*, Stroud, Sutton Publishing, 1997

Howe, Bea. *A Galaxy of Governesses*, London, Derek Verschoyle, 1954

Hughes, Kathryn. *The Victorian Governess*, London and Rio Grande, Hambledon Press, 1993

Peterson, M. Jeanne. 'The Victorian Governess: Status Incongruence in Family and Society' in Marth Vicinus (ed.) *Suffer and Be Still: Women in the Victorian Age*, Bloomington, Indiana University Press, 1972, pp. 3–19

Pitcher, Harvey. *When Miss Emmie Was In Russia*, London, John Murray, 1977

Poovey, Mary. *Uneven Developments: The Ideological Work of Gender in Mid-Victorian Britain*, London, Virago, 1989

Renton, Alice. *Tyrant or Victim? A History of the British Governess*, London, Weidenfeld and Nicolson, 1991

Tannahill, Reay. *Sex in History*, London, Hamish Hamilton, 1980

Thomson, Patricia. *The Victorian Heroine: A Changing Ideal, 1837–1873*, Oxford, OUP, 1956

West, Katherine. *Chapter of Governesses: A Study of the Governess in English Fiction, 1800–1949*, London, Cohen, 1949

INDEX